OECD DOCUMENTS
OCDE

CURRICULUM REFORM
ASSESSMENT IN QUESTION

LA RÉFORME DES PROGRAMMES SCOLAIRES
L'ÉVALUATION EN QUESTION

PUBLISHER'S NOTE

The following texts have been left in their original form to permit faster distribution at lower cost. The views expressed are those of the author(s).

NOTE DE L'ÉDITEUR

Les textes reproduits ci-dessous ont été laissés dans leur forme originale pour permettre, pour un coût moindre, une diffusion plus rapide. Les vues exprimées n'engagent que leur(s) auteur(s).

CENTRE FOR EDUCATIONAL RESEARCH AND INNOVATION
CENTRE POUR LA RECHERCHE ET L'INNOVATION DANS L'ENSEIGNEMENT

ORGANISATION FOR ECONOMIC CO-OPERATION AND DEVELOPMENT
ORGANISATION DE COOPÉRATION ET DE DÉVELOPPEMENT ÉCONOMIQUES

ORGANISATION DE COOPÉRATION ET DE DÉVELOPPEMENT ÉCONOMIQUES

En vertu de l'article 1er de la Convention signée le 14 décembre 1960, à Paris, et entrée en vigueur le 30 septembre 1961, l'Organisation de Coopération et de Développement Economiques (OCDE) a pour objectif de promouvoir des politiques visant :

— à réaliser la plus forte expansion de l'économie et de l'emploi et une progression du niveau de vie dans les pays Membres, tout en maintenant la stabilité financière, et à contribuer ainsi au développement de l'économie mondiale ;
— à contribuer à une saine expansion économique dans les pays Membres, ainsi que les pays non membres, en voie de développement économique ;
— à contribuer à l'expansion du commerce mondial sur une base multilatérale et non discriminatoire conformément aux obligations internationales.

Les pays Membres originaires de l'OCDE sont : l'Allemagne, l'Autriche, la Belgique, le Canada, le Danemark, l'Espagne, les Etats-Unis, la France, la Grèce, l'Irlande, l'Islande, l'Italie, le Luxembourg, la Norvège, les Pays-Bas, le Portugal, le Royaume-Uni, la Suède, la Suisse et la Turquie. Les pays suivants sont ultérieurement devenus Membres par adhésion aux dates indiquées ci-après : le Japon (28 avril 1964), la Finlande (28 janvier 1969), l'Australie (7 juin 1971) et la Nouvelle-Zélande (29 mai 1973). La Commission des Communautés européennes participe aux travaux de l'OCDE (article 13 de la Convention de l'OCDE).

Le Centre pour la Recherche et l'Innovation dans l'Enseignement a été créé par le Conseil de l'Organisation de Coopération et de Développement Economiques en juin 1968.

Les principaux objectifs du Centre sont les suivants :

— *encourager et soutenir le développement des activités de recherche se rapportant à l'éducation et entreprendre, le cas échéant, des activités de cette nature ;*
— *encourager et soutenir des expériences pilotes en vue d'introduire des innovations dans l'enseignement et d'en faire l'essai ;*
— *encourager le développement de la coopération entre les pays Membres dans le domaine de la recherche et de l'innovation dans l'enseignement.*

Le Centre exerce son activité au sein de l'Organisation de Coopération et de Développement Economiques conformément aux décisions du Conseil de l'Organisation, sous l'autorité du Secrétaire général et le controle direct d'un Comité directeur composé d'experts nationaux dans le domaine de compétence du Centre, chaque pays participant étant représenté par un expert.

© OCDE 1993

Les demandes de reproduction ou de traduction totales ou partielles de cette publication doivent être adressées à :
M. le Chef du Service des Publications, OCDE
2, rue André-Pascal, 75775 PARIS CEDEX 16, France.

FOREWORD

This report is the third in a series of publications emanating from CERI's programme on School Reform and Innovations in Learning. The other two volumes, *Curriculum Reform - An Overview of Trends* (OECD/CERI, 1990) and *Learning to Think -- Thinking to Learn* (OECD/CERI, Pergamon Press, 1991) covered a broad spectrum of developments in OECD countries - the first volume being concerned with current trends in curriculum reform and the second with advances that have been made in the state of knowledge about how children learn to think and reason.

In this volume selected examples of assessment in schools in seven OECD countries are analysed. It is concluded that assessment procedures are crucial in shaping the process of learning and in achieving the objectives of the stated curriculum.

This volume, as well as those mentioned above, provides an important background to the OECD Conference on "The Curriculum Redefined -- Schooling for the 21st Century" (Paris, 5-8 April 1993).

The report, prepared by John Nisbet, is published on the responsibility of the Secretary-General of the OECD but the views expressed are those of the authors and do not commit either the Organisation or the national authorities concerned.

AVANT-PROPOS

Ce rapport est le troisième de la série de publications du CERI sur "La réforme de l'école et les innovations dans l'enseignement". Deux précédents volumes, *La réforme des programmes scolaires : Où en sommes nous ?* (OCDE/CERI, 1990) et *Apprendre à penser, penser pour apprendre* (OCDE/CERI, 1993), couvrent un large éventail d'innovations mises en oeuvre dans les pays de l'OCDE. Le premier est consacré aux récentes réformes des programmes scolaires, l'autre, aux progrès des connaissances sur les mécanismes de pensée et de raisonnement des enfants.

Ce volume présente des exemples d'évaluations réalisées dans les écoles de sept pays de l'OCDE, et montre que les méthodes d'évaluation sont essentielles pour bien orienter le processus d'apprentissage et atteindre les objectifs assignés aux programmes scolaires.

Cet ouvrage, et les deux précédents, servira de toile de fond aux discussions de la Conférence de l'OCDE sur "La redéfinition des programmes : L'enseignement pour le XXIe siècle" (Paris, 5-8 avril 1993).

Ce volume, préparé par John Nisbet, est publié sous la responsabilité du Secrétaire général de l'OCDE. Les opinions avancées sont celles des auteurs et n'engagent en rien l'Organisation ou les autorités nationales concernées.

CONTENTS/SOMMAIRE

Résumé (in French).. 7

CHAPTER 1: Introduction
    by *John Nisbet*.. 25

CHAPTER 2: France
    by *Patricia Broadfoot*... 39

CHAPTER 3: Germany/Allemagne
    by *Margaret Sutherland*.. 53

CHAPTER 4: The Netherlands/Pays-Bas
    by *Margaret Sutherland*.. 67

CHAPTER 5: Spain/Espagne
    by *John Nisbet*.. 79

CHAPTER 6: Sweden/Suède
    by *Margaret Sutherland*.. 91

CHAPTER 7: The United Kingdom/Royaume-Uni
    by *Caroline Gipps*... 105

CHAPTER 8: The United States of America/Etats-Unis
    by *John Nisbet*.. 121

CHAPTER 9: Issues/Questions
    by *John Nisbet*.. 137

RÉSUMÉ

Au sein de l'école moderne, l'évaluation influe de manière décisive sur le mode d'apprentissage des élèves et sur le comportement pédagogique des enseignants. Qu'elle intervienne pour les examens et pour les tests, ou bien pour la notation et le passage dans la classe supérieure, elle est omniprésente. Elle fausse parfois le processus d'apprentissage en axant l'enseignement sur l'examen, le bachotage, la mémorisation à court terme, l'anxiété et le stress, au point que l'objectif de la réussite à l'examen prend autant d'importance que le processus même d'acquisition des connaissances que l'examen est censé évaluer. De nombreux jeunes ont le sentiment que l'évaluation exerce une dictature sur l'enseignement. "J'ai l'impression d'avoir passé ma vie en examens", nous confiait un jeune étudiant espagnol que nous avons interrogé.

Les partisans d'une réforme en sont parfois arrivés à demander la suppression des examens. On imagine mal toutefois une suppression totale de toute forme d'évaluation, car le terme d'évaluation a une acception plus large que celui d'examen. L'évaluation fait intégralement partie de l'apprentissage. Encore faut-il qu'elle soit conçue de manière adéquate du point de vue des modalités, de l'utilisation, du niveau de difficulté, de la fréquence, du calendrier et du retour de l'information pour qu'elle exerce un effet positif sur l'apprentissage. En tant qu'apprenant, on a besoin d'information sur sa propre performance, de manière à voir ce qui a été maîtrisé et ce qui ne l'a pas été, mais aussi pour orienter et stimuler la poursuite du processus. Lorsque l'investissement personnel diminue, l'évaluation devient un outil permetttant de donner une nouvelle motivation et de canaliser les efforts. Les gens qui veulent véritablement apprendre et qui ne disposent pas de batteries de tests standardisés, se testent eux-mêmes par tâtonnements successifs, à moins qu'ils ne sollicitent les commentaires informels de leur enseignant, de leur employeur, de leurs clients ou de leurs pairs, de manière à contrôler l'état d'avancement de leurs connaissances. Mais lorsque la chose est possible, il importe que le processus d'évaluation devienne explicite, objectif et systématique. Ce qu'il faut, disent les plus modérés, c'est réformer l'évaluation, non la faire disparaître.

Outre ce rôle de formation et de diagnostic, l'évaluation joue d'autres rôles qui sont importants dans une société moderne : elle assure la sélection là où une sélection est indispensable et elle garantit une compétence. Le recrutement pour un travail, une formation ou un cycle d'études spécialisées doit s'appuyer sur la manifestation irréfutable d'une compétence et d'une aptitude.

Il est évident que ce rôle de certification est important. Quand on exerce une activité qualifiée comportant des responsabilités, qu'on soit conducteur de véhicule, gestionnaire de fonds publics ou chirurgien, on ne peut dénier à la collectivité le droit de procéder à un contrôle prélable de la compétence. Dans une telle optique, le test (ou l'examen formel) présente un certain nombre d'avantages : il est apparemment plus objectif, plus équitable et plus ouvert qu'une appréciation personnelle subjective, surtout si cette appréciation émane de ceux qui sont intervenus directement dans la formation. Mais il comporte également un biais, dans la mesure où il suppose la définition d'un seuil minimum de performance. Il tend donc à influer directement sur le contenu de la formation, par l'intermédiaire de programmes axés sur cette évaluation, et par là même à influer sur la méthode d'enseignement et le mode d'apprentissage (comme le montre bien, par exemple, la préparation à l'examen du permis de conduire). Si le contrôle des connaissances est bien fait et complet, tout va bien : on peut s'en servir pour élever le niveau, ou du moins pour contrôler les contenus et les méthodes. Si ce contrôle n'est pas bien fait, il peut avoir des effets très réducteurs sur les contenus ; et dans la mesure où les tests sont généralement courts et sélectifs, et où ils s'intéressent souvent par priorité à ce qui se mesure facilement (ou de manière fiable), ils comportent un réel risque.

Le rôle de certification joué par les tests est largement reconnu et rares sont ceux qui le contesteraient (sauf peut-être pour déplorer leur caractère insuffisamment sélectif). Mais si l'on poursuit le raisonnement et si on l'applique à l'ensemble du processus éducatif, on se rend compte qu'on ne peut se contenter de vérifier le niveau de compétence en fin de processus et qu'il faut au contraire le vérifier périodiquement en cours de processus. Le fait qu'on se préoccupe beaucoup depuis quelques années du niveau des connaissances exigibles a modifié la conception de l'évaluation, notamment celle de l'examen national, qui permet de contrôler l'efficacité du système, mais aussi d'introduire les notions de transparence et de contrôle. Il s'ensuit que dans de nombreux pays développés on considère désormais qu'il convient de vérifier le niveau des exigences et qu'il y a là un véritable impératif politique. On peut parler d'impératif politique dans la mesure où il s'agit de garantir une transparence et un contrôle, et donc de contribuer à imposer des programmes nationaux avec l'intention d'élever le niveau de base.

Les diverses attentes formulées à l'égard du processus d'évaluation semblent donner l'assurance que toute une gamme de contrôles et d'examens se maintiendront dans un avenir prévisible. Les questions qui se posent sont nombreuses : quelles sont les formes d'évaluation les mieux adaptées aux différentes fonctions ? Un même examen peut-il remplir différentes fonctions ? Ces fonctions sont-elles compatibles entre elles et, dans le cas contraire, à laquelle faut-il donner la priorité ? Quelles en seront les incidences sur l'enseignement et l'apprentissage ? De nombreux facteurs incitent à modifier les programmes : les nouveaux progrès en science et en technologie, les exigences nouvelles en matière de maîtrise des langues étrangères, les nouvelles méthodes d'enseignement et des conceptions nouvelles de l'apprentissage. L'évolution des valeurs et des attentes de la société, l'augmentation de l'offre d'éducation sont également sous-jacentes à ce besoin de changement : c'est ainsi que l'expansion brutale de l'enseignement du second degré au cours de la seconde moitié du XXe siècle a créé un besoin de réforme au niveau des programmes traditionnels et des examens finaux du second degré qui préparaient l'entrée à l'université pour une petite élite.

Face à cette pression, les systèmes d'évaluation font preuve d'une extraordinaire inertie. Pour qu'une proposition de réforme aboutisse, il faut qu'il y ait changement dans les attitudes du public et des milieux professionnels et que les points de vue évoluent en ce qui concerne la fonction des examens et la nature des aptitudes testées. Chaque pays a sa propre "culture d'évaluation", c'est-à-dire un ensemble de pratiques élaborées au fil des ans, liées à des valeurs très ancrées, qui garantissent (comme toute culture) la continuité et la stabilité indispensables, mais qui d'un autre côté résistent souvent obstinément et de manière irrationnelle à toute idée de changement.

Etant donné que l'évaluation détermine dans une large mesure le contenu de l'enseignement et de l'apprentissage, il importe qu'elle soit intégrée par avance dans toute réforme des programmes. Si l'on redéfinit les programmes sans prendre en compte l'omniprésence de l'évaluation, on se condamne selon toute vraisemblance à l'inefficacité : enseignants et élèves auront tendance à répondre aux exigences explicites de la méthode d'évaluation plutôt qu'à la rhétorique des déclarations d'intention. Mais on peut également retourner l'argument : si l'évaluation influe sur le contenu de l'enseignement et de l'apprentissage, pourquoi ne pas profiter de l'occasion pour faire en sorte que cette influence s'exerce dans le bon sens ? En faisant de l'évaluation un élément à part entière de la réforme des programmes, on peut s'en servir pour atteindre certains des objectifs du programme en favorisant (voire en exigeant) un style d'apprentissage qui coïncide avec ces objectifs. On peut sans doute envisager d'introduire des modèles d'évaluation qui aideraient à mettre en oeuvre la réforme des programmes considérée comme souhaitable.

Une telle stratégie est toutefois risquée : elle peut aboutir à un programme centré sur l'évaluation, avec tous les effets réducteurs et inhibants qui l'accompagnent, si l'évaluation est mal conçue. En particulier dès que l'enjeu devient important, dès que les décisions cruciales concernant l'élève sont prises en fonction de résultats d'examens, l'évaluation peut parfaitement modeler le programme, en fixer les objectifs et déterminer les aspects du savoir et de l'aptitude qui auront la priorité (et qui seront perçus par l'enseignant et l'élève comme importants). On reproche souvent aux méthodes traditionnelles d'évaluation de trop privilégier la mémorisation et la reproduction, au détriment de la résolution de problèmes, du raisonnement critique et de la pensée créatrice. Les procédures d'évaluation méritent donc d'être revues de manière à accorder la place qui leur revient aux aptitudes et aux compétences intéressant la société contemporaine, et valorisées par elle, même s'il est malaisé de mettre au point des méthodes permettant de les mesurer. Analysant l'incidence de l'évaluation sur l'apprentissage, Crooks (1988) énonce une règle d'or :

> "Le message le plus substantiel qui émane de ce travail est l'idée qu'en tant qu'éducateurs nous avons à faire en sorte d'accorder, dans notre activité d'évaluation, l'importance qu'ils méritent aux aptitudes, aux savoirs et aux comportements que nous considérons comme vraiment décisifs. Les résultats seront sans doute parfois difficiles à évaluer, mais il importe que nous trouvions les moyens permettant de les évaluer."

L'évaluation serait-elle alors capable d'induire par ce biais un changement ? Les examens nationaux sont considérés (par ceux qui les défendent) comme un moyen d'élever le niveau, surtout si l'on publie la moyenne des notes obtenues dans les établissements ou au niveau du district, de manière à pouvoir faire pression lorsque les notes tombent au-dessous de la moyenne nationale.

Certains mettent en doute l'efficacité de cette utilisation de l'évaluation comme outil de "transparence". C'est ainsi que Stake (1990) s'en prend à "la vision optimiste selon laquelle la mesure fournit une base d'information pour l'amélioration de la qualité scolaire". La mesure (terme plus restrictif qu'évaluation) permet de voir si les résultats se situent au-dessus ou au-dessous de la norme, mais ne disent pas comment améliorer la performance. Certains examens nationaux comportent un élément de diagnostic (ou peuvent être utilisés à des fins de diagnostic) : il s'agit de repérer les parties du programme pour lesquelles les résultats sont médiocres (par rapport à la moyenne nationale ou à d'autres parties du programme) et donc d'orienter le travail de l'enseignant. Mais on a affaire là à une forme de pression plutôt brutale qui ignore les différences individuelles.

Il importe que l'évaluation aille au-delà de la mesure ; il faut qu'elle guide l'élève dans son effort d'amélioration de la performance, qu'elle nourrisse et qu'elle modèle l'enseignement. On parle parfois en l'occurrence du rôle "formatif" de l'évaluation et les adeptes de ce point de vue souhaiteraient que l'évaluation devînt partie intégrante du processus éducatif, car ils y voient un facteur normal de l'interaction entre l'apprenant et l'enseignant et entre l'apprenant et le contenu. Si l'on veut que l'évaluation ainsi comprise améliore l'enseignement, il convient soit de redéfinir les méthodes traditionnelles de test et d'examen en prenant comme critère leur rôle dans l'apprentissage et dans l'enseignement, soit de les modifier ou de les remplacer de manière à leur faire jouer un rôle positif. C'est bien là le principe qui sous-tend ce qu'on appelle le mouvement pour une "évaluation alternative", qui se manifeste en particulier aux Etats-Unis et qui trouve un large écho dans d'autres pays (quoique sous une dénomination différente).

Glaser (1990) résume ainsi le propos :

"Nous sommes tous pleinement conscients du fait que l'évaluation des résultats obtenus par l'élève, telle qu'elle est pratiquée dans les écoles, avec les devoirs sur table et toute la gamme des contrôles, influe sur les objectifs éducatifs du système et, par voie de conséquence, sur la transmission culturelle des savoirs de chaque discipline ; ce sont les examens qui décident de ce que nos enfants apprennent et qui disent s'ils sont bien préparés pour l'avenir. Le résultat de ces évaluations retentit également sur l'auto-évaluation des apprenants, sur leurs aspirations, sur leur investissement personnel dans l'étude et donc, en fin de compte, sur les qualités d'esprit que leur génération finit par valoriser. L'évaluation et l'examen ont une telle influence sur la vie que si l'on ne se préoccupe pas de leur incidence et si l'on ne les aborde pas sous un angle nouveau, on passe à côté d'une possibilité majeure d'amélioration de l'éducation."

Le programme CERI/OCDE

Le présent ouvrage a pour origine un programme de cinq ans du Centre pour la recherche et l'innovation dans l'enseignement (CERI) de l'OCDE. Ce programme, intitulé "Réforme des programmes d'étude et efficacité de l'enseignement" passe en revue les évolutions récentes et les développements possibles dans les programmes d'étude des Etats Membres de l'OCDE. Il couvre toute une série de domaines, regroupés en cinq sous-projets :

- i) Apprendre à penser -- penser pour apprendre (thème d'une conférence de 1989) ;
- ii) Enseignement des sciences, des mathématiques et de la technologie (thème d'une conférence de 1990) ;
- iii) Le tronc commun ;
- iv) Sciences humaines et valeurs morales ;
- v) Evaluation.

Les rapports émanant de ces différents projets seront regroupés dans un rapport final et dans une conférence sur "La redéfinition des programmes d'étude" qui se tiendra en 1993. Bien qu'abordée en dernier, l'évaluation n'est pas une pièce rapportée. Une réforme de l'évaluation ne peut venir qu'après une décision sur les programmes d'étude, mais une réforme des programmes d'étude implique une redéfinition de l'évaluation, de manière à faire passer dans les faits les réformes proposées et à supprimer les éléments de démotivation. Trop de propositions de réforme s'enlisent du fait qu'elles se heurtent à des procédures d'évaluation qui les contrarient ou bien, plus fondamentalement, parce qu'elles entrent en conflit avec une "culture de l'évaluation" solidement ancrée. Toutefois, le Comité directeur des programmes CERI considère la réforme de l'évaluation comme autre chose qu'une simple suppression des barrières : la conception de l'évaluation est absolument décisive pour la mise en forme du processus d'apprentissage et pour atteindre les objectifs des programmes d'étude remodelés.

Les préoccupations concernant le niveau et le recours à un système national d'examen pour contrôler l'offre d'enseignement constituent l'autre thème central qui s'est dégagé lors de la discussion préliminaire du Comité directeur. Parmi les nombreux changements intervenus dans le système éducatif des pays Membres de l'OCDE, l'introduction d'un examen national a été l'un des faits significatifs des dernières années. Ce point a donné lieu à des interprétations différentes selon les pays : dans certains cas, notamment au Royaume-Uni et aux Etats-Unis, l'examen national a reçu un traitement privilégié au sein de la réforme de l'éducation (ce qui a suscité des remous dans l'opinion) ; d'autres pays ont instauré un examen national, mais en lui donnant un rôle d'appoint, relativement subalterne.

Compte tenu de ces thèmes, sept pays dans lesquels il existe un programme national de réforme ou dans lesquels on a enregistré des évolutions marquantes en matière d'évaluation de l'enseignement se sont vu confier un rapport : Allemagne, Espagne, Etats-Unis, France, Pays-Bas, Royaume-Uni et Suède. Les visites de ces pays ont eu lieu d'avril à juin 1991 et les rapports ont été rédigés en juillet 1991. Ces rapports nationaux sont présentés dans les chapitres qui suivent. Ils ne prétendent pas à l'exhaustivité : il a été demandé aux auteurs de se concentrer sur deux thèmes principaux et de respecter des consignes draconiennes en matière de longueur des textes. Les changements dans ce domaine interviennent à un rythme tellement rapide que quelques mois après la rédaction de ces rapports, on signalait déjà de nouvelles évolutions ; mais les questions soulevées restent tout à fait d'actualité.

Thèmes centraux

On peut les résumer de la manière suivante :

1. Le contrôle du niveau national, nouvel impératif politique : utilisation de l'évaluation aux fins de contrôle et de transparence pour les systèmes nationaux, avec notamment une évaluation à l'échelon national des acquis des élèves en ce qui concerne les compétences de base et les matières principales ;

2. Nouvelles approches de l'évaluation, substitution de modèles avec intégration de l'évaluation dans l'enseignement : contrôle continu visant à apprécier le travail permanent des élèves plutôt qu'examen formel ou test standardisé, fiches personnelles, dossiers, tâches pratiques, évaluation au sein de l'établissement par les enseignants et auto-évaluation des élèves, les résultats étant utilisés rétroactivement pour définir les objectifs et inciter les apprenants à prendre en charge leur propre apprentissage.

Le thème 1 semble contradictoire avec le thème 2 : ce dernier est privilégié par les professionnels de l'éducation, alors que le premier trouve un large écho auprès des hommes politiques, des parents et des responsables administratifs. Il s'ensuit qu'il existe un divorce idéologique entre ceux qui voudraient élever le niveau en étendant le système de l'examen et ceux qui voudraient améliorer la qualité de l'apprentissage en modifiant les méthodes d'évaluation. La solution consiste peut-être à reconnaître que ces deux axes de développement ont chacun leur intérêt et à s'efforcer de les concilier en posant que l'évaluation a des fonctions multiples et qu'elle doit donc être multiforme. Un tel compromis a toutefois son point faible : dans la mesure où l'évaluation implique parfois de très gros "enjeux", comme lorsqu'on fait appel à elle pour prendre des décisions importantes concernant l'avenir des élèves évalués -- ce qui est le cas quand il y a sélection, délivrance d'un diplôme ou publication des résultats d'un examen national --, cet aspect de l'évaluation l'emportera très vite sur ses autres fonctions, là où "l'enjeu" est moins important et où il s'agit simplement d'apporter un élément d'information, sans jugement définitif.

On peut sans doute résoudre de manière plus constructive ce conflit entre les deux finalités de l'évaluation, la fonction de "transparence" et la fonction de "formation", en cherchant à les réunir au sein d'un même système d'évaluation. Cela implique la mise au point d'un examen national incitant à adopter des formes nouvelles, plus adaptées, d'apprentissage et prenant en compte, pour répondre au besoin de contrôle national, de nouvelles formes d'évaluation "formative". Nous distinguons ici deux niveaux d'utilisation de l'évaluation : évaluation du système et évaluation du processus. Le premier relève de la responsabilité des autorités qui ont à contrôler l'efficacité du système et des établissements. Le second, qui utilise l'évaluation en tant qu'outil d'aide et d'information pour l'apprentissage et l'enseignement, relève essentiellement de la responsabilité des enseignants et des apprenants eux-mêmes. Le problème est de savoir si ces deux fonctions sont compatibles ou au contraire inconciliables.

Thème 1. Niveau national

L'évaluation du niveau scolaire national constitue désormais un nouvel impératif politique alors que jusqu'ici on pensait qu'il s'agissait uniquement d'un problème professionnel et pédagogique. La revendication n'est pas nouvelle : au XIXe siècle, il a été créé des inspections nationales et des examens nationaux en contrepartie de l'effort financier consenti par l'Etat pour l'éducation universelle. Mais depuis peu on accorde de plus en plus d'importance aux examens nationaux, et ce pour toute une série de raisons : augmentation constante des coûts de l'éducation, inquiétude sur les aptitudes de base en lecture et en écriture de certains élèves sortant du système, demande d'une élévation des qualifications pour des raisons de développement économique national, et exigence de transparence formulée par les parents et l'opinion publique vis-à-vis du corps enseignant. On a donc tendance à considérer les examens nationaux comme une méthode de contrôle de l'offre d'éducation permettant de couvrir certains secteurs, fixés à l'avance, du savoir et de la compétence. On fait également valoir que les résultats d'une évaluation à l'échelon national peuvent fournir un retour d'information utile pour les enseignants, les élèves, les parents et les responsables administratifs et donc contribuer à assurer la tâche prioritaire, à savoir l'élévation du niveau national.

Mis à part ce problème très général, qui est de savoir si les examens nationaux constituent la meilleure méthode pour améliorer le niveau, il existe d'autres questions plus particulières qui intéressent le débat : sur quels éléments l'examen doit-il porter ? A quel âge ou à quel point du cursus doit-il être organisé ? Selon quelle méthode et quels critères la décision doit-elle être prise dans ce domaine ?

Un examen à l'échelon national doit obligatoirement porter sur les aptitudes de base. Mais là encore, on peut se demander si cet examen doit se limiter à la "compétence minimale" ou bien couvrir une gamme plus large de savoir-faire. Car outre les aptitudes de base, il serait bon de vérifier les acquis dans certaines matières (en sciences notamment). L'esthétique et le développement moral ou personnel représentent certes des aspects importants de la formation, mais il est difficile d'en évaluer les acquis à l'aide de méthodes standardisées. Il est plus commode d'apprécier l'acquis cognitif que la compréhension, de vérifier si l'élève reproduit correctement le cours que de voir s'il est capable d'une réflexion créatrice ou critique. Mais si l'on parvient à mettre au point des tests adéquats, un système d'examen national pourrait parfaitement se révéler capable de garantir que les programmes correspondent effectivement aux priorités éducatives convenues.

A quel âge faire passer cet examen ? L'idée d'un examen national en fin de scolarité obligatoire conçu comme l'un des éléments de la sanction des études, indispensable dans une société développée, est généralement bien acceptée. Mais à ce stade du cursus, il est déjà trop tard pour de nombreux élèves. Il s'ensuit que la plupart des projets envisagent un examen pour chaque année, ou sinon un sondage à certains stades du cursus. La date du premier examen est un sujet controversé, dans la mesure où un examen national trop précoce risque de "coller une étiquette" à l'élève, ce que certains considèrent comme allant à l'encontre de la philosophie générale du début de la formation. De manière plus positive, on peut utiliser l'examen pratiqué à divers stades du cursus pour cerner la "progression" dans certains domaines du programme, l'hypothèse étant qu'il existe un itinéraire optimal pour parvenir à la maîtrise et à la compréhension.

Les modalités de l'examen constituent de toute évidence un problème central. On admet généralement que les examens formels peuvent avoir un effet réducteur et l'on met en doute leur validité et leur fiabilité. Les questionnaires à choix multiple sont suspects dans la mesure où ils font appel à la mémoire et où ils impliquent une fragmentation du savoir. Pour répondre à ces objections, il conviendrait d'élaborer de nouvelles formes de contrôle permettant d'apprécier la compréhension, la capacité de mobiliser ses connaissances, ainsi que le sens critique et le raisonnement créatif. Mais il existe également un fort mouvement (voir Thème 2) en faveur du recours à des dossiers de niveau, avec fiches individuelles détaillées, et appréciation de l'acquis dans plusieurs domaines de compétence, pour remplacer la note ou le bilan de l'année scolaire. Cela implique qu'on fasse davantage appel aux appréciations des enseignants, surtout pour les aspects essentiels du cursus pour lesquels il n'est pas possible de faire des contrôles objectifs. Toutefois, les dossiers de niveau ne fournissent pas les indications chiffrées indispensables pour comparer les élèves et les établissements (alors que c'est là précisément l'argument qu'invoquent les partisans de ce système) et ils posent problème au niveau de l'enregistrement et de la communication des résultats. On peut envisager de combiner l'évaluation interne et l'évaluation externe en utilisant l'examen formalisé pour "pondérer" (fournir des termes de comparaison avec) les appréciations des enseignants de l'établissement.

Il convient de préciser les critères à retenir pour parvenir à une prise de décision. Si l'évaluation est censée appuyer le programme d'études et non le régenter, il convient de la juger en fonction de sa capacité ou de son incapacité d'atteindre les objectifs déclarés du programme. Est-il possible d'élaborer des systèmes d'évaluation qui aideraient à atteindre les résultats souhaités ? Crooks (1988) résume son analyse exhaustive des incidences de l'évaluation sur les élèves en se référant aux objectifs essentiels :

> "Il importe de faire de l'apprentissage en profondeur un objectif central de l'éducation et d'avancer sur cette voie en se servant de l'évaluation des élèves. Cela implique que l'on privilégie la compréhension, le transfert de savoir au profit de questions ou de situations nouvelles, ainsi que d'autres aptitudes intellectuelles et que le développement de ces aptitudes soit évalué par le recours à des tâches qui fassent clairement appel à d'autres facultés que la reconnaissance ou la mémoire."

Il faut donc expliciter la logique de l'examen national et aller au-delà des déclarations rhétoriques en faisant passer cette logique dans son élaboration et dans l'utilisation de ses résultats. Nous avons parlé de "gros enjeu" pour caractériser la situation dans laquelle les résultats scolaires ont une incidence immédiate sur les perspectives d'avenir des élèves et des enseignants : là, l'examen dicte sa loi aux programmes et ignore la rhétorique. Si les enseignants se montrent réticents, c'est en partie parce qu'ils redoutent ce type d'examen "couperet", examen trop limité qui introduit une distorsion dans les programmes, pénalise les élèves et les établissements de zones défavorisées, favorise "l'étiquetage" et la démotivation et sert de manière détournée à juger les enseignants. Parler d'examen "à faible enjeu" serait maladroit car l'expression implique l'idée d'évaluation anodine ; en réalité, il s'agit d'une conception dans laquelle l'évaluation se soumet à la loi des programmes ; elle devient pour l'enseignant comme pour l'élève une affaire de jugement personnel. Les partisans de l'examen national assimilé à un impératif politique exigent que l'évaluation soit un processus public, l'idée étant que l'enseignement est quelque chose de trop important pour qu'on le confie aux enseignants.

Nouvelles approches de l'évaluation

Examens et contrôles traditionnels ne trouvent plus guère de défenseurs. Bien que l'attitude de rejet et de méfiance vis-à-vis des examens formels s'explique souvent par des raisons plus profondes, les examens s'exposent à un certain nombre de reproches en raison de leur caractère artificiel (la base d'appréciation est trop étroite), leur manque de fiabilité (écarts entre les notes données par différents examinateurs et entre les résultats de l'élève), leur absence de validité (importance excessive de la technique d'examen, de la mémoire et de l'expression écrite), et surtout leur rôle réducteur en matière d'apprentissage et d'enseignement. Toutefois, les examens assurent un certain nombre de fonctions indispensables : formation, bilan final, diagnostic et évaluation, orientation, filtrage, sélection et certification ; et on admet en général leur caractère impartial, par opposition à la note de l'enseignant qui prête parfois le flanc à la critique.

Toutefois, depuis le début des années 60, on note une tendance générale à faire davantage confiance à l'évaluation interne de l'établissement, à donner en ce domaine plus de responsabilités aux enseignants, voire aux apprenants eux-mêmes par le biais de l'auto-évaluation ou de l'évaluation collégiale par les pairs. Si notre objectif consiste à élaborer un système d'évaluation intégrant la qualité et améliorant l'enseignement et l'apprentissage, sa réalisation dépendra dans une large mesure des enseignants. C'est la raison pour laquelle, même si l'éducation est quelque chose de trop important pour qu'on la confie aux enseignants, il n'en demeure pas moins que le rôle des enseignants est trop important pour qu'on le néglige.

L'évaluation interne comprend l'évaluation, par l'enseignant, du travail de l'année ainsi que des examens internes, dont les résultats peuvent toutefois être modérés par des intervenants extérieurs ou combinés à des tests chiffrés visant à éviter les distorsions. Le travail de développement réalisé sur les dossiers de niveau (le profil de l'élève) s'efforce d'aboutir à une forme plus structurée, mais aussi plus complexe, d'évaluation qui tient compte de la complexité de la performance scolaire, et qui fait souvent appel à une appréciation portée en fonction d'un certain nombre de critères, plutôt qu'à un classement fondé sur une norme. L'évaluation interne passe pour avoir un certain nombre d'avantages dans la mesure où elle donne un meilleur retour d'information pour l'élève comme pour l'enseignant, où elle est plus susceptible de créer une motivation et où elle réduit la tentation d'un enseignement axé sur l'examen. Il reste toutefois cetains problèmes à régler avant qu'on puisse faire entièrement confiance à l'évaluation interne, même repensée, pour élever le niveau de l'enseignement.

La première question et la plus générale concerne le lieu où s'exerce le contrôle. Si l'on considère que l'évaluation est un moyen de vérifier le contenu de l'enseignement, un système interne délègue une grande partie de ce pouvoir à l'école elle-même. On peut se demander si cette évaluation serait considérée comme crédible par l'opinion publique ; par ailleurs, les comptes rendus de l'évaluation risquent de ne pas donner aux familles le genre de renseignements qu'elles souhaitent recevoir. Un système "mixte" d'évaluation interne et externe assorti de directives générales sur les programmes et sur la modération des évaluations scolaires serait sans doute plus conforme aux attentes du public. Mais ces deux modalités d'évaluation sont-elles compatibles ? Comment combiner une évaluation descriptive, sans jugement, sans "étiquetage", avec des notes comparables, communicables et normalisées ? Dans une situation où l'enjeu est élevé, ce sont les exigences des examens et des tests extérieurs qui risquent de l'emporter.

Se pose en outre la question pratique de la mise en oeuvre. L'évolution de l'évaluation extérieure représente une longue histoire, et ses techniques sont connues et comprises par les enseignants, les élèves et le public. En revanche, les techniques de l'évaluation interne ne sont pas encore parfaitement au point, ni acceptées par le public, encore qu'il ne faille pas sous-estimer l'éventuel changement de cadence de l'évolution des attitudes du public à l'égard de l'enseignement. Ce sont des procédures qui imposent une charge de travail importante aux enseignants et nécessitent donc des ressources et des formations supplémentaires.

Les rapports des pays qui figurent aux chapitres suivants décrivent diverses tentatives visant à améliorer l'efficacité de l'évaluation et à en réduire les effets secondaires indésirables. On peut dire que ces nouvelles approches représentent trois niveaux de réforme qui vont du changement minime à la réforme radicale :

Utiliser des procédures diverses répondant à la diversité des fonctions qu'on attend de l'évaluation (A) ;

Instaurer des modifications qui s'appliquent aux méthodes d'examen et de test en vigueur (B) ;

Adopter une approche radicalement neuve visant à intégrer l'évaluation à l'enseignement (C).

A. L'évaluation doit remplir des fonctions multiples : il paraît donc tout à fait logique de faire appel à *une gamme plus large de techniques d'évaluation*, adaptées chacune à une fonction : les tests standardisés pour apprécier le niveau et la transparence ; les tests de diagnostic pour l'orientation ; une combinaison d'examens externes et internes et le contrôle continu au sein de l'établissement pour la délivrance des diplômes ; les dossiers de niveau ou les dossiers personnels pour les parents et les employeurs potentiels, et ainsi de suite. C'est une démarche qui est suivie dans de nombreux pays et il ne s'agit donc pas d'une approche nouvelle : la nouveauté réside dans la possibilité de mobiliser et d'utiliser effectivement cette gamme de méthodes. Pour illustrer ce point, on peut prendre l'exemple du Fonds commun d'outils d'évaluation mis en place dans l'Ontario (voir chapitre 8). Ce système distingue l'évaluation initiale, l'évaluation formative et le bilan de scolarité ; pour chacune de ces fonctions, il offre une série de techniques, tests, entretiens, outils d'auto-évaluation, objectifs, listes de contrôle et techniques d'observation (avec indication des critères retenus et des indicateurs à suivre), mais aussi blocs didactiques pouvant servir d'aides à l'évaluation.

Cette solution de compromis présente deux grandes faiblesses : elle augmente la charge d'examen et elle risque de privilégier une forme d'examen (celle qui est liée aux "gros enjeux") au détriment des autres. Dans l'idéal, on souhaiterait une stratégie plus cohérente (et plus économique) dans laquelle un plan d'évaluations combinées remplirait toutes les fonctions de manière efficace ; mais beaucoup d'experts de l'évaluation sont d'avis que cet idéal est hors de portée ou même fallacieux.

B. Il existe une autre procédure communément adoptée, celle qui consiste à *modifier les méthodes d'évaluation traditionnelles*. C'est ainsi que dans tous les pays où il existe un examen national pour la délivrance du diplôme de fin d'études du second degré, on a procédé au cours des dernières années à un aménagement de cet examen (voir chapitres 2, 3, 4, 5 et 7). Cet aménagement a consisté à introduire une évaluation, interne à l'établissement, de projets de quelque envergure, à tenter de tester (et donc de favoriser) la résolution de problèmes et la mobilisation des connaissances, à évaluer les aptitudes pratiques et les aptitudes en matière d'expression orale, et à instaurer un lien étroit entre les examens et un certain nombre d'objectifs définis de manière précise.

Aux Etats-Unis et dans les autres pays ayant largement recours aux tests standardisés (notamment aux Pays-Bas et en Suède), le caractère réducteur qu'on attribue généralement aux QCM a conduit à utiliser plus généreusement les questions à réponse libre qui exigent un effort de rédaction. On propose des sujets plus complexes, afin d'éviter le caractère fragmentaire des tests à réponses brèves : on demande aux élèves de rédiger un court exposé pour prouver leur capacité de résoudre les problèmes, interpréter des données, tirer des conclusions et organiser leur argumentation ; et les contrôles de lecture portent sur des textes plus longs, voire sur des ouvrages figurant au programme de la classe. Les questions sont formulées de manière à contraindre l'élève à une réflexion autonome et à "un effort intellectuel soutenu" (Wolf *et al.*, 1991) au détriment des réponses toutes prêtes.

Ces aménagements ne font pas l'unanimité. Les tentatives de réforme des examens finaux se heurtent souvent à de fortes résistances : en 1984, une manifestation a réuni dans les rues de Paris trois millions d'opposants à un projet de réforme de l'enseignement (voir chapitre 2). La modification des systèmes de tests standardisés suscite deux types de reproche : l'introduction de la dimension subjective dans la notation et la charge de travail supplémentaire impliquée.

La subjectivité affecte la fiabilité des notations, rend la comparaison entre établissements plus malaisée et expose au reproche de parti pris. Le recours à des grilles de référence comportant un échantillonnage de performances scolaires est l'une des solutions envisageables : le Programme de notations de référence de Toronto en est un exemple raffiné.

Se pose également la question de la charge de travail supplémentaire imposée aux enseignants par cette démarche, qui est plus longue. Les enseignants peuvent se dire que leur temps serait mieux employé à enseigner plutôt qu'à évaluer. On peut escompter cependant qu'à la longue l'introduction de systèmes informatisés permettra peut-être de réduire les coûts et de simplifier le traitement des données. En matière d'évaluation informatisée, les principaux développements ont porté sur les tests standardisés, avec mise en place de banques de questions et d'un ingénieux système de notation automatique des questions à choix multiple : citons l'utilisation de grilles de correction pour les questions comportant des réponses chiffrées, le système de réponse "figurative" dans lequel l'élève trace des flèches pour indiquer la bonne direction, fait un point pour repérer la localisation, interprète des données et dessine des graphiques, le tout pouvant être lu optiquement, analysé et noté par l'ordinateur. L'informatique aide également à établir des dossiers, à stocker et à rappeler des données individuelles précises et à produire des rapports individuels sur les élèves. A un autre niveau, l'ordinateur peut proposer des tests interactifs dans lesquels les questions sont "faites sur mesure" de manière à pouvoir s'adapter au niveau de l'élève, avec feedback immédiat et enregistrement des réponses. Toutefois, il ne faudrait pas que la technologie progresse beaucoup plus vite que les applications pratiques, sinon elle risque de ne pas être adoptée. Les systèmes sophistiqués ont tendance à exclure tous les non-initiés ; et il y a place pour des sytèmes moins puissants, qui seront vraisemblablement utilisés par le plus grand nombre, dans un premier temps du moins. L'informatique peut s'imposer dans la mesure où elle réduit les coûts et où elle se montre plus efficace : Broadfoot (1990) remarque que l'efficacité tend à être valorisée par rapport à la rentabilité. Le premier critère d'évaluation des procédures nouvelles est leur incidence sur l'apprentissage.

C. Murphy (1990; voir aussi chapitre 8 dans ce volume) considère qu'à ce deuxième niveau de réforme on vise simplement à "faire des aménagements", alors qu'au troisième niveau on opère une véritable "refonte". Dans de nombreux pays, il existe un mouvement très puissant, soutenu notamment, mais pas exclusivement, par les milieux professionnels, en faveur d'*une redéfinition de l'évaluation*. Ici, on ne fait plus de distinction entre évaluation et formation : l'évaluation n'est plus un élément artificiel et étranger, elle fait intégralement partie de l'enseignement. L'évaluation formative canalise les interactions entre enseignants et élèves : dans le bilan scolaire, elle assigne des objectifs à l'enseignement et à l'apprentissage. Encore que apparue à une date relativement récente dans le contexte scolaire, cette philosophie est bien connue en formation continue et en formation des adultes, dans l'apprentissage ouvert et dans le télé-enseignement, ainsi que dans les schémas d'auto-enseignement (on parle parfois d'apprentissage souple).

Les termes évaluation "authentique", évaluation "formative" et évaluation "alternative" visent tous le même ensemble de méthodes d'évaluation à incidence positive sur l'enseignement et l'apprentissage, celles qui contribuent à la réalisation des objectifs éducatifs, qui définissent des tâches proches de la vie réelle ("authentiques") et qui s'intéressent prioritairement aux contenus et aux savoir-faire pertinents, en se modelant pour l'essentiel sur les tâches incluses dans le processus normal d'apprentissage en classe. Lorsque les tâches d'évaluation sont ainsi en phase avec les contenus et les objectifs de l'enseignement, le fait d'enseigner dans la perspective de l'examen et d'étudier pour atteindre le niveau d'exigence de l'examen devient quelque chose de positif et de valable. C'est là, disent certains, le vrai moyen d'élever le niveau. L'examen obligatoire vise à élever indirectement le niveau, mais par le biais de l'exigence de transparence : or une progression de la moyenne des notes obtenues aux contrôles peut parfaitement ne traduire chez l'élève qu'une amélioration fallacieuse de l'aptitude à passer des tests. L'évaluation authentique vise à élever directement le niveau en améliorant l'enseignement et l'apprentissage, en établissant un lien étroit entre l'examen et l'enseignement, de manière à ce que son incidence sur le travail en classe soit bénéfique, du moins le souhaite-t-on.

On parle parfois d'évaluation "alternative" pour désigner un aménagement du système traditionnel de test évoqué ci-dessus (niveau 2) ; mais en règle générale, le terme se démarque beaucoup plus nettement du système classique d'examen. Dwyer (1990) évoque : "une substitution totale de modèles (paradigm shift) pour aller d'une méthode qui privilégie la prévision et le contrôle à une méthode qui privilégie le sens et la compréhension". Wolf et al. notent ceci : "L'élaboration et la mise en oeuvre de ces formes nouvelles d'évaluation n'implique rien de moins que le passage définitif de ce que nous appelons une 'culture du test' à une 'culture de l'évaluation'."

La frontière entre réforme radicale et simples aménagements reste incertaine : une série d'aménagements mineurs est parfois indispensable avant que ne se produisent des changements radicaux d'attitude. Au sens étroit, l'évaluation alternative implique le recours à des fiches personnelles, à des dossiers de niveau, à des profils d'élève, ainsi qu'au contrôle continu et à des modules d'enseignement comportant une définition des objectifs et des critères d'évaluation (voir chapitre 5). Au sens large, l'évaluation alternative inclut l'auto-évaluation, la possibilité pour l'élève d'apprécier son propre niveau et d'utiliser cette appréciation à la fois comme diagnostic et comme outil de formation de manière à améliorer les stades ultérieurs de l'apprentissage, ce point étant considéré comme l'un des objectifs prioritaires de l'éducation. L'évaluation alternative prend notamment en compte l'élément affectif de l'apprentissage, elle sait l'importance d'une bonne attitude psychologique vis-à-vis de l'acte d'apprendre et l'intérêt qu'il y a à créer une bonne ambiance scolaire ; elle connaît le rôle-clé des rapports humains, de l'image qu'on a de soi-même et de la perception de la tâche. (Ces points sont abordés de manière plus détaillée au chapitre 9).

Une telle conception s'expose à deux grands reproches visant, d'une part, les ressources supplémentaires qu'elle implique, d'autre part, sa crédibilité auprès de l'opinion publique. L'évaluation alternative n'est pas facile à mettre en place. Elle exige davantage d'efforts que l'examen traditionnel, et non l'inverse ; elle est donc plus coûteuse en termes de temps humain et de travail de formation, aussi bien pour les enseignants que pour les élèves. Plus encore, elle implique un profond changement d'attitude qui pour l'instant n'enthousiasme guère le corps enseignant, les parents ou l'opinion publique. Elle ne fournit pas de données vraiment concrètes sur la performance des élèves (bien que les renseignements qu'elle fournit soient sans doute plus "valables"), sur le niveau respectif des établissements, des enseignants, et des élèves pris individuellement. Elle déplace le lieu du contrôle, et elle délègue une grande partie de ses pouvoirs aux enseignants et aux établissements. Il existe également des problèmes de notation, mais la notation n'est pas la fonction principale de l'évaluation alternative. La méthode traditionnelle d'examen est jugée sur sa validité et sur sa fiabilité, deux termes qu'il convient de redéfinir si on veut les appliquer à l'évaluation alternative (voir chapitre 8) : on dira par exemple que la validité d'une mesure se juge à ses effets sur l'apprentissage, à sa capacité d'améliorer l'acquisition des connaissances et des aptitudes définies au niveau des objectifs du programme d'études. Messick (1989) suggère l'introduction du terme de "validité induite" pour désigner l'incidence de l'examen sur l'enseignement en classe.

Questions

Il avait été demandé aux auteurs des rapports nationaux présentés dans les chapitres qui suivent de se concentrer sur deux thèmes centraux, à savoir l'examen national et les nouvelles méthodes d'évaluation, ainsi que de repérer les problèmes qui se posent. Ces rapports soulèvent plusieurs questions concrètes concernant l'application des stratégies d'évaluation. Les responsables ont tendance à faire confiance aux chercheurs, dont ils attendent des éléments d'information sur lesquels fonder leurs décisions : celles-ci doivent, comme il est naturel, s'inscrire dans le cadre de la politique nationale existante. Toutefois, un coup d'oeil d'ensemble révèle à quel point ces politiques nationales peuvent diverger entre elles, ce qui soulève nécessairement des questions d'une autre ampleur.

Tels sont les conflits qui sous-tendent nos attentes vis-à-vis de l'évaluation. Les préoccupations actuelles s'expliquent par le mécontentement de l'opinion publique vis-à-vis de l'offre d'enseignement (d'où les pressions en faveur d'un examen national et d'une appréciation du travail des enseignants et une plus forte implication des parents), ainsi que par les critiques émanant des milieux professionnels à l'encontre des procédures d'examen traditionnelles (qu'on voudrait remplacer pour instaurer un lien plus étroit entre l'enseignement et l'évaluation et donner plus d'autonomie aux enseignants). Ces attitudes contradictoires ne se laissent pas facilement harmoniser.

L'évaluation remplit deux grandes fonctions, elles aussi difficiles à concilier :

-- Elle mesure la performance des apprenants pris individuellement, des établissements et du système dans son ensemble (fonction associée à l'attestation de compétence, à la transparence et au contrôle) ;

-- Elle est composante à part entière du processus d'apprentissage (par retour d'information, orientation, diagnostic des difficultés, définition des objectifs et motivation).

Pour la première de ces deux fonctions, l'évaluation peut être dite externe, dans la mesure où elle utilise, pour mesurer la performance, des critères extérieurs au processus d'apprentissage. Il s'agit là d'une évaluation qui se réfère généralement à des normes et qui se traduit souvent par un diplôme, une notation ou un classement. Pour la seconde, l'évaluation peut être dite essentiellement interne, en ce sens que le résultat auquel elle parvient n'a de valeur que s'il est reconnu par l'apprenant lui-même : il s'agit là d'une évaluation généralement fondée sur des critères et mettant l'accent sur la maîtrise des contenus d'enseignement. Le conflit entre ces deux fonctions est l'une des causes du dilemme qui surgit lorsqu'on doit assigner une place et des modalités à cette évaluation au sein de nos sytèmes éducatifs.

Le facteur décisif ne réside pas tant dans le test lui-même que dans les conséquences du résultat : il peut y avoir "gros enjeu" ou "faible enjeu". C'est donc la place de l'évaluation dans la globalité du système éducatif qui pose problème, et pas uniquement son contenu ou ses modalités. En matière d'évaluation, les vraies questions sont stratégiques, et non pas techniques : il s'agit moins de trouver le test idéal que de décider de l'utilisation des résultats. Les deux aspects sont naturellement interdépendants : les modalités peuvent déterminer ou restreindre l'utilisation.

Il existe également un conflit virtuel entre les modèles qui sous-tendent les différentes méthodes d'évaluation. Le modèle par objectifs, qui a actuellement les faveurs de la planification éducative, fixe un certain nombre d'objectifs à atteindre et leur donne un caractère contraignant, à la fois pour les élèves et pour les enseignants. Le modèle inspiré par la théorie constructiviste de l'apprentissage, qui a pris beaucoup d'importance au cours des 20 dernières années, insiste au contraire sur l'idée de prise en compte d'aspirations auxquelles les apprenants eux-mêmes peuvent s'identifier. S'il s'agit d'un problème de responsabilité, s'il s'agit de savoir à qui incombent en dernière analyse les décisions concernant le contenu et les limites des programmes scolaires, à l'Etat, aux enseignants ou aux apprenants eux-mêmes, alors on peut dire raisonnablement qu'il y a là une responsabilité partagée et que dans l'idéal chacun devrait faire en sorte de soutenir l'action des autres.

Le rapport annuel de 1990 du Service des examens de l'éducation nationale aux Etats-Unis se montre optimiste lorsqu'il croit détecter :

"... un certain consensus, au sein de ce qu'on pourrait appeler 'le mouvement pour la réforme des examens', quant à la direction dans laquelle il conviendrait de s'engager si l'on veut que les examens permettent d'atteindre des objectifs éducatifs." (ETS, 1990).

Il y a consensus sur l'idée que la fonction "formative" de l'évaluation est extrêmement importante et l'on ose espérer que ce point de vue n'est pas uniquement celui du mouvement pour la réforme des examens. Hargreaves (1989) résume bien le point lorsqu'il décrit l'évaluation "comme un élément de l'apprentissage plutôt que comme un jugement porté sur la performance, une fois le cours terminé."

Glaser (1990) va plus loin lorsqu'il parle de l'évaluation en termes de "moyen d'acquisition" :

"Pour mettre l'examen au service de l'apprentissage, il faut favoriser l'instauration d'un environnement dans lequel l'examen soit considéré comme un moyen de mesurer les compétences humaines indispensables à la formation ultérieure plutôt que comme un moyen de mesurer un acquis passé ou actuel. Une fois bien maîtrisés, les savoirs et les compétences acquis dans un domaine devraient être considérés comme des moyens d'acquisition de compétences ultérieures... Cette idée de moyen d'acquisition incite à évaluer le savoir en fonction de son utilisation constructive dans une démarche ultérieure. La question que devrait poser l'examen est celle-ci : l'étudiant est-il en mesure d'utiliser ses acquis actuels pour poursuivre son travail d'information, d'apprécier des faits, de juger d'une performance esthétique, de comparer différentes stratégies d'action, d'organiser ses idées et de prendre des décisions argumentées ?"

REFERENCES

BROADFOOT, P. (1990), Communication personnelle.

CROOKS, T.J. (1988), "The Impact of classroom evaluation practices on students", *Review of Educational research*, 58 (4), 438-481.

DWYER, C.A. (1990), "Trends in the assessment of teaching and learning: Educational and methodological perspectives", dans Broadfoot, P., Murphy, R. et Torrance H. (dir. publ.) *Changing Educational Assessment: International perspectives and trends*. Londres : Routledge.

EDUCATIONAL TESTING SERVICE (1990), *Helping America Raise Educational Standards for the 21st Century: 1990 Annual Report*. Princeton: ETS.

GLASER, R. (1990), "Toward new models for assessment", *International Journal of Educational Research*, 14 (5), 475-483.

HARGREAVES, A. (1989), *Curriculum and Assessment Reform*. Milton Keynes: Open University Press.

MESSICK, S. (1989), "Validity", dans Linn, R. L. (dir. publ.), *Educational measurement* (3e édition). New York: Macmillan.

MURPHY, J. (dir. publ.) (1990), *The Educational Reform Movement of the 1980s*. Berkeley: McCutchan.

STAKE, R. (1990), Communication personnelle.

WOLF, D., BIXBY, J., GLEEN, J. III et GARDNER, H. (1991), "To use their minds well: Investigating new forms of student assessment", *Review of Research in Education*, 17, 31-74.

Chapter 1

INTRODUCTION

by
Professor John Nisbet
University of Aberdeen

In today's schools, assessment is a main influence on how pupils learn and how teachers teach. Whether assessment is in the form of examinations and tests, or marks and grades for course work, its influence is pervasive. Often it distorts the process of learning, through teaching to the test, cramming, short-term memorising, anxiety and stress - to the extent that learning to cope with examinations has become almost as important as the genuine learning which these examinations are supposed to measure. For many young people, assessment dominates education. "I seem to have spent my whole life in examinations" said one young student from Spain whom we interviewed.

Consequently some radical reformers have argued for the abolition of examinations. Few, however, would argue for abolishing assessment of every kind, for "assessment" is a more general term than "examination". Assessment is part of learning; but it must be appropriately designed, in terms of form, use, level of difficulty, frequency, timing, and feedback, if it is to make a positive contribution to learning. As learners, we need information on our performance as a check on what we have or have not mastered, and as a guide and stimulus to subsequent learning. When interest is minimal, testing provides a leverage to stir motivation and channel efforts. If we really want to learn and there are no formal tests, we test ourselves by trial and error, or use the informal comments of teacher, employer, clients or peers to assess our progress. Where possible, then, let us make the process of assessment explicit, objective and systematic. What is needed, say the moderates, is to reform the assessment system, not to abolish it.

In addition to these formative and diagnostic functions of assessment, there are other functions which are of importance in a modern society: to select when a choice has to be made, and to certify competence. Selection for jobs, for training, or for specialised courses of study, should be based on attested evidence of competence and suitability.

The certification function is clearly of value. Those who perform any skilled and responsible job - drive a car, administer public funds, operate as a surgeon - must accept society's claim to exercise a prior check on competence. For this purpose, a formal test or examination has the advantages of objectivity, apparent fairness and openness, in comparison with personal private judgement, especially if that judgement is made by those who have been closely involved in previous training. But there is a side effect, since the examination defines a minimum standard for acceptance; and thus it tends to define the content of the training -- an assessment-led curriculum -- and influences both the method of teaching and the style of learning. (Preparing for a driving test is an illustration of this process.) If the test is well designed and comprehensive, this may be all to the good: it provides a means of raising standards, or at least exercising control over content and method in the curriculum. If the test is inadequate, its effect on the curriculum can be seriously limiting; and since tests are usually short and selective and often concentrate on what is most easily (or reliably) measured, this is a real danger.

The certification function of testing is accepted so generally that few would question it (except perhaps to complain that it is not sufficiently discriminating). But if we follow up this line of reasoning and apply it to the whole educational process, we see that standards are not something just to be assessed at the end, but at intervals throughout the process. Concern over standards in education in recent years has introduced a new element in the assessment scene, national testing, which not only provides a check on the effectiveness of the system but also introduces accountability and control. Consequently, the use of tests to monitor standards in schools has become a political imperative in many developed countries. It is political in the sense that its purpose lies in establishing accountability and control, helping to impose a prescribed national curriculum with the aim of raising basic standards.

The many functions which assessment is required to perform would seem to guarantee the continuance of various forms of testing and examinations for the foreseeable future. There are many questions at issue: What forms of assessment are best suited for the different functions? Can one style of examination perform different functions? Are the functions compatible, if not, which should have priority? What effect does all this have on teaching and learning? There are many pressures for change in the curriculum: new developments in science and technology, new requirements for fluency in foreign languages, new methods of teaching and new insights into learning. Changes in values and expectations in society, and the growth of educational provision, underlie this pressure for change: for example, the massive expansion of secondary education in the second half of the 20th century created a need for reform of a traditional curriculum and college-oriented certificate examinations designed for a minority elite.

In the face of these pressures for reform, assessment systems show a remarkable resistance to change. Any proposal for reform depends on changing public and professional attitudes and assumptions about the functions of examinations and the nature of ability. Each country has its own "assessment culture", a body of practices established over time and linked with deeply held values, which (like other cultures) provide a necessary continuity and stability but are strongly and often irrationally resistant to change.

Because assessment is a powerful determinant of what is taught and learned, there is a need to plan assessment as an integral element in curriculum reform. Redefining the curriculum without taking account of the pervasive influence of assessment is likely to be ineffective: teachers and pupils alike will tend to work to the reality of requirements as outlined by the form of assessment rather than to the rhetoric of a statement of intent. But the point can be made more positively if we turn the argument round: since assessment influences what is taught and learned, why not turn that to advantage, so that the influence is in the direction we want? Assessment planned as an integral element in curriculum reform can contribute to achieving curriculum objectives, by encouraging (or even requiring) a style of learning in line with these objectives. Perhaps we can introduce new models of assessment which will help to implement the curriculum reforms which we see as desirable.

This strategy, however, runs the risk of setting up an assessment-led curriculum with a limiting or inhibiting effect unless assessment is well designed. Especially in a "high stakes" context, where crucial decisions for individual pupils are made on the results of testing, assessment can readily drive the curriculum, shaping the goals and determining which aspects of knowledge and skill are treated as important (and perceived by pupils and teachers as important). Traditional methods of assessment are often criticised as placing over-emphasis on memory and recall, neglecting problem-solving, critical reasoning and creative thinking. Assessment procedures therefore need to be redesigned to give proper place to the skills and competences which are most relevant and valued in today's society, even if it proves difficult to devise means of measuring them. Crooks (1988), reviewing the impact of assessment on students' learning, expresses a guiding principle:

> "The most vital of all the messages emerging from this review is that as educators we must ensure that we give appropriate emphasis in our evaluations to the skills, knowledge and attitudes that we perceive to be most important. Some of these important outcomes may be hard to evaluate, but it is important that we find ways to assess them."

But can assessment operate as a lever for change in this way? For example, national testing is seen (by those who argue for it) as a means of raising standards, especially if average scores for schools or districts are made public, to apply pressure on those who fall below the national average. The effectiveness of this "accountability" use of assessment is challenged by some critics. Stake (1990), for example, queries "the optimistic belief that measurement provides an informational platform for improving school quality". Measurement (a narrower term than assessment) shows whether achievement is above or below the norm, but not how to improve performance. Some national testing includes a diagnostic element (or can be used diagnostically) to identify aspects of the curriculum where performance is poor (relative to the national average or to other aspects of the curriculum) and thus to direct teaching effort. But this is a relatively crude form of pressure, insensitive to individual differences.

Assessment should go beyond measurement, guiding pupils on how to improve their performance, informing and shaping learning. This is sometimes called the "instructional" use of assessment, and those who argue for this approach seek to make assessment an integral part of the educational process, seeing it as a natural element in the interaction between learner and teacher and between learner and content. If assessment is to improve education in this way, traditional methods of testing and examining require to be reviewed against the criterion of their influence on learning and teaching, and modified or replaced so that their influence is benevolent. This is the underlying principle of the "alternative assessment" movement, particularly evident in the United States and widely accepted in other countries (though not under that banner).

Glaser (1990) sums up the argument:

"We are all keenly aware that the assessments of student achievement that the schools use -- classroom tests and large-scale testing programs -- shape the educational goals that drive the system and, thus, the cultural transmission of disciplinary knowledge; tests determine what our children learn and how well they are prepared for the future. The results of these assessments also influence how students assess themselves, what they aspire to, and how much effort they put into their activities, and thereby, ultimately, the qualities of mind that their generation comes to value. Assessment and testing so strongly influence our lives that, unless we examine their impact and consider new approaches to their design, we neglect a major opportunity to improve education."

The CERI/OECD programme

This book has its origins in a five-year programme of the Centre for Educational Research and Innovation (CERI) of the OECD. This programme, under the heading of "Curriculum reform and school effectiveness" reviews recent changes and potential developments in the school curricula of the OECD Member states. It covers a range of aspects, grouped in five sub-projects:

i) Learning to think -- thinking to learn (the theme of a 1989 conference);
ii) Science, mathematics and technology (a 1990 conference theme);
iii) The core curriculum;
iv) Humanities and values;
v) Assessment.

The reviews from these projects will be brought together in a final report and conference on "The curriculum redefined" in 1993. Assessment comes last in this series; but not as an after-thought. Reform of assessment comes after decisions about curriculum, but curriculum reform has to include rethinking assessment, to help implement proposed changes and to remove disincentives. Too many proposals for reform founder because they come up against an inimical assessment procedure -- or, more fundamentally, because they clash with an established "assessment culture". But the Steering Committee of the CERI programme viewed the reform of assessment as more than the removal of barriers: the design of assessment is crucial to shaping the process of learning and to achieving the objectives of "the curriculum redefined".

Concern over standards and the use of national testing to monitor educational provision was the other central theme which emerged in preliminary discussion in the Steering Committee. Among the many changes in assessment procedures in the education systems of OECD Member states, the introduction of national testing is one distinctive feature of recent years. The concept has been interpreted in different ways in different countries: in some -- the United Kingdom and the United States, for example -- national testing has been given an important role in educational reform (and has met with public controversy); in other countries, national testing has been introduced with a supportive but relatively subordinate function.

Consequently, with these themes in mind, reports were commissioned on seven countries where there have been national programmes of reform or distinctive developments in educational assessment: France, Germany, the Netherlands, Spain, Sweden, the United Kingdom and the United States of America. Visits to these countries were made in April-June 1991, and the reports were written in July 1991. These country reports are presented in the chapters which follow. They do not claim to be comprehensive reviews: the authors were asked to focus on the two key themes and were given a severe limit on length. Such is the pace of change in this field that within a few months of the completion of these reports, there were new developments to report; but the issues which are raised in the reports are still highly topical.

Key themes

The two themes may be summarised thus:

1. Testing national standards, a new political imperative: the use of assessment for monitoring and accountability in national systems, especially in terms of nation-wide testing of pupils' achievement in basic skills or core subjects of the curriculum;

2. New approaches to assessment, a paradigm shift towards integrating assessment with learning: continuous assessment using pupils' regular work rather than formal examinations or standardized tests, records of achievement, portfolios, practical tasks, school-based assessment by teachers and self-assessment by pupils, using results as feedback to help define objectives and encourage learners to take responsibility for their own learning.

Theme 1 may be seen as in conflict with Theme 2, the second being favoured by the professionals in education, against pressure for the first from politicians, parents and administrators. As a result, there is an ideological divide between those who hope to raise standards by more extensive testing and those who hope to improve the quality of learning by changing assessment methods. The answer may be to acknowledge the strength of both lines of development and seek to proceed with both approaches, recognising that assessment has multiple functions and therefore should adopt a variety of forms. The weakness of this compromise is that, if certain functions of assessment are perceived as involving "high stakes" -- where the results are used to make important decisions affecting those being assessed, as in selection, certification and national testing where results are published -- these will quickly come to dominate the "low stakes", supportive, non-judgemental forms of assessment.

A more constructive resolution of the conflict between the two uses of assessment, the "accountability" use and the "instructional" use, is to seek to combine both within a single system of assessment. This implies designing national testing to encourage new or improved styles of learning and adapting new forms of instructional assessment to provide for national monitoring. Here, we are distinguishing two levels in the use of assessment in education:

assessment of the system and assessment of the process. The first of these is a responsibility of the providing authorities to monitor the efficiency of the system and of schools within the system. The second is the use of assessment formatively to support and inform learning and teaching, a responsibility primarily of teachers and of the learners themselves. The issue is whether these two functions are compatible, or are they fundamentally irreconcilable?

Theme 1. National standards

The assessment of national standards of educational attainment is a new political imperative in what formerly was seen as primarily a professional and pedagogical concern. It is not a new demand: in the 19th century, national inspectorates were formed and national examination systems introduced as a consequence of state expenditure on universal education. But recent years have seen increased emphasis on schemes of national testing, for a variety of reasons: escalating costs of education, dissatisfaction with the basic literacy and numeracy of some school-leavers, demand for improved skills for national economic development, and the insistence that the teaching profession should be more accountable to parents and public. Thus, national testing tends to be seen as a method of monitoring and control of educational provision, ensuring adequate coverage of prescribed areas of knowledge and skill. There is also the argument that the results of national assessment can provide useful feedback to teachers, students, parents and administrators, and thus will help to fulfil the prime aim, to raise educational standards nationally.

In addition to the broad question of whether national testing is the best way to raise standards, there are specific issues for debate: what aspects should be tested, at what ages or stages, by what methods and by what criteria do we decide on these issues?

National testing must include basic skills, but even here there is the question whether assessment should be limited to "minimum competency" or cover a wider range of achievement. Beyond the basic skills, attainment in specific subject areas (science, for example) should be monitored. Aesthetic studies and personal or moral development are important aspects of education, but are difficult to assess in a standard form. It is easier to test knowledge than understanding, and to test accuracy in reproducing what has been taught rather than creative and critical reasoning. But if appropriate tests can be designed, a system of national testing might provide an effective means of ensuring that the curriculum truly reflects the agreed priorities for education.

At what ages should tests be applied? National assessment at the end of the compulsory years of schooling is widely accepted as part of the function of certification required in a developed society. By that stage, it is too late for many students. Consequently, most schemes of national testing cover the whole age range, or sample at stages throughout. How early tests should begin is a matter of controversy, since early testing may have a "labelling" effect and is seen by some as at odds with the philosophy of early education. More positively, testing at different stages can be used to delineate "progression" through a defined area of the curriculum, on the assumption that there is a standard best route to mastery and understanding.

Method of testing is clearly a crucial consideration. The restrictive influence of formal examinations is widely recognised, and their validity and reliability are often challenged. Multiple-choice tests are suspect insofar as they depend on recognition and involve fragmentation of knowledge. Developing new forms of testing to measure understanding, application of knowledge, and critical and creative reasoning would meet this criticism. But there is a strong movement (see Theme 2) towards the use of records of achievement -- detailed profiles for individual pupils, identifying mastery over a range of attainment instead of a score or grade -- relying more on teachers' assessments, especially for important aspects of the curriculum which cannot be tested objectively. However, records of achievement do not yield the numerical grades necessary for comparison of students and institutions (which their advocates see as an argument in favour), and they raise problems of recording and communication. It is possible to envisage a combination of external and internal assessment in which formal testing is used to "moderate" (provide comparability between) teachers' internal assessments.

The criteria for decision on these issues need to be specified. If assessment is to support and not drive the curriculum, it should be judged by whether it helps to achieve or defeat the declared objectives of the curriculum. Can we design national assessment systems which will help towards the desired outcomes? Crooks (1988) summarises his extensive review of the impact of evaluation on students by reference to prime objectives:

> "There is a need to make deep learning a central goal of education, and to foster development of this goal through the evaluation of students. This requires that we place emphasis on understanding, transfer of learning to untaught problems or situations, and other thinking skills, evaluating the development of these skills through tasks that clearly must involve more than recognition or recall."

Thus the rationale of national testing must be made explicit, not just as rhetoric but implemented in the design and in the use to be made of the results. The term "high stakes" is used to describe testing where results directly influence pupils' and teachers' prospects: this kind of testing drives the curriculum irrespective of rhetoric. Resistance from teachers is partly suspicion of "high stakes" testing, on too limited a base and thus distorting the curriculum, unfair to pupils and schools in disadvantaged areas, leading to labelling and discouraging, and as a disguised form of appraisal of teachers. "Low stakes" testing is an unfortunate term if it implies lack of importance; properly it implies a use of assessment which is subordinate to the curriculum, a private judgement personal to pupil and teacher. The political imperative underlying the demand for national assessment insists that assessment should be public, on the argument that education is too important to be left to the teachers.

Theme 2. New approaches to assessment

Traditional examinations and tests have few friends. Though there are often deep reasons for the dislike and fear of formal examinations, they are open to criticism on several grounds: their artificiality (too limited a basis for judgement), unreliability (variation between markers and in pupils' performance), lack of validity (over-dependence on examination technique, memory and writing skill), and primarily the limiting influence of examinations on learning and teaching. However, examinations perform a range of necessary functions, formative, summative, diagnostic and evaluative, for guidance, reporting, screening, selection and certification; and they are widely accepted as impartial, in contrast to teachers' marks which are less easily defended against complaints of bias.

However, a general trend since the 1960s has been the greater reliance on internal school assessment, giving greater responsibility for assessment to teachers, and even to the learners themselves through self-assessment or peer-assessment. If our aim is to design an assessment system which is integrated with and helps to improve the quality of teaching and learning, the fulfilment of that aim will depend largely on the teachers. Therefore, though education is too important to be left to the teachers, it is also true that the teachers' contribution is too important to be neglected.

School-based assessment uses the teachers' assessment of course work and examinations set internally within schools, though the results may be moderated by external assessors or combined with test scores to guard against bias. Development work on records of achievement (or profiles) has attempted to provide a structured but more complex form of assessment which does justice to the complexity of scholastic performance, often through criterion-referenced statements rather than norm-referenced grading. The advantages claimed for internal assessment are that it provides better information for guidance and feedback to pupils and teachers, that it is more likely to generate motivation, and that it reduces the temptation to teach to the test. However, there are issues which require to be resolved before we can confidently look to improved internal assessment to raise educational standards.

The first and most general issue concerns the locus of control. If the assessment system is seen as a means of controlling the content of education, a school-based system delegates much of this power to the individual school. It is open to question whether such assessment would command public credibility; and records of achievement may not provide the kind of information which parents seek. A "mixed" system of internal and external modes of assessment, with broad guidelines on curriculum and moderating of school assessments, is more likely to meet public expectations. But are the two modes of assessment compatible? How do we combine descriptive, non-judgemental, non-labelling assessment with comparable, communicable, standardized grades? In a "high stakes" situation, the requirements of external tests and examinations are likely to prove dominant.

There is also the practical issue of implementation. External assessment has a long history of development and its techniques are known and understood by teachers, students and public. The techniques of internal assessment are not yet fully developed or publicly accepted -- though we should not underestimate the possible pace of change in public attitudes to education. The procedures place a substantial burden of work on teachers, and therefore require additional resources and training.

The country reports in the following chapters describe a variety of attempts to improve the efficiency and reduce undesirable side-effects of assessment. These new approaches can be categorised as representing three levels of reform, ranging from minimal change to radical reform:

- Using a variety of procedures for the variety of functions which assessment is required to perform (A);

- Introducing modifications to established methods of examining and testing (B);

- Adopting a radical new approach which aims to integrate assessment with learning (C).

A.   Since assessment has to perform a diversity of functions, there is a strong case for using a greater *variety of techniques*, each serving a particular function: standardized tests for measuring standards and accountability; diagnostic tests for guidance; a combination of external examinations and internal school continuous assessment for certification; records of achievement or portfolios for reporting to parents and potential employers; and so on. This is the practice adopted in most countries, and consequently is not a new approach: the novel element is the availability and use of such a variety of methods. An example to illustrate is the Ontario Assessment Instruments Pool (see Chapter 8). This resource distinguishes initial assessment, formative assessment and summative evaluation, and for each of these functions offers a range of techniques -- tests, interviews, self-assessment instruments, targets, checklists and observation (with guidelines on criteria and indicators to note) -- as well as curriculum resource units to be used to assist in assessment.

There are two main weaknesses in this compromise solution: the resulting increased burden of testing, and the risk that one form of testing (that which carries the "highest stakes") will dominate all the others. Ideally, one would hope for a more coherent (and more economical) policy, in which one combined pattern of assessment would perform all the necessary functions with equal success; but many writers on assessment regard this ideal as unattainable, or even as a misguided aspiration.

B.   Another commonly adopted procedure is to *introduce modifications* to established methods of assessment. For example, in every country which has a national examination for certification towards the end of secondary education, these examinations have been extensively revised in recent years (see chapters 2, 3, 4, 5 and 7). The modifications have included school-based assessment of extended projects, attempts to test (and thus foster) problem-solving and the application of knowledge, assessing practical ability and oral communication skills, and relating examinations more precisely to clearly stated objectives.

In the United States and other countries which make extensive use of standardized tests (such as the Netherlands and Sweden), the widely acknowledged limitations of multiple-choice items have led to modifications in the type of questions asked in tests. There is wider use of open-ended questions which require a constructed response. More complex tasks are set, to avoid the fragmentation of short-answer tests: students are asked to write brief essays to demonstrate their ability to solve problems, interpret data, draw conclusions and organise logical arguments; and tests of reading use longer passages or even books from the students' course work. Test questions are designed which require students to think independently and which "model sustained thoughtfulness" (Wolf *et al.*, 1991) rather than routine responses.

These changes are not universally supported. Attempts to reform long-established certificate examinations often meet with strong resistance: in 1984 three million people demonstrated on the streets of Paris in protest against proposed educational reforms (see Chapter 2). Changes in standardized testing encounter two main lines of criticism: the introduction of subjectivity in marking and the extra labour involved.

Subjectivity lowers reliability of marking, makes comparability between schools more difficult, and opens the way for complaints of bias. The use of reference scales of samples of pupils' performance is one method of dealing with this problem: the Toronto Benchmarks Program (see Chapter 8) is a sophisticated example.

There is also the question of the extra work for teachers involved in applying these new procedures. They are time-consuming, and teachers may feel that their time is better spent in teaching than in assessment. There is a hope that, in time, the introduction of computerised systems of assessment may be able to reduce costs and simplify the information processing. The main developments in computerised assessment have been with standardized tests, in compiling data banks of test items and machine scoring of multiple-choice tests where ingenious procedures have been introduced: for example, the use of grids for numerical answers, and "figural responses" in which students draw arrows to indicate direction, make marks to indicate location, interpret data and sketch graphs, which can be scanned, analysed and scored by computers. Computers also help in reporting, in the storage and retrieval of detailed records, and in producing computerised individual reports on students. At a more advanced level, computers can offer new forms of interactive testing, in which the questions are "tailored" to adjust to the performance level of the student, with instant feedback and a cumulative record. But the technology should not run too far ahead of implementation, or it may not be taken up. Sophisticated systems tend to exclude all but the initiated; and there is a case for low-powered systems which more people are likely to use, initially at least. Computerised systems may be adopted because they are more efficient in reducing costs, or because they are more effective in achieving aims: Broadfoot (1990) notes that efficiency tends to be elevated over effectiveness. The prime criterion for evaluating innovatory procedures is their impact on learning.

C. Murphy (1990; see also Chapter 8 in this volume) describes this second level of reform as "repair": the third level he describes as "redesign". There is a strong movement in many countries, supported mainly but not exclusively by professional groups, for a *radical new approach to assessment*. In this approach, the distinction between assessment and instruction is removed: assessment is not an artificially separate event but an integral part of instruction. In formative assessment it guides the interaction of teacher and student; in summative assessment it identifies objectives for teaching and learning. This approach, though still relatively novel in the school context, is familiar enough in adult and continuing education, in open learning and distance learning, and in schemes of supported self-study (sometimes described as flexible learning).

The terms "authentic assessment", "instructional assessment" and "alternative assessment" are all used to refer to methods of assessment which influence teaching and learning positively in ways which contribute to realising educational objectives, requiring realistic (or "authentic") tasks to be performed and focusing on relevant content and skills, essentially similar to the tasks involved in the regular learning processes in the classroom. When assessment tasks are thus brought into line with instructional content and aims, then teaching to the test and studying to meet test requirements become constructive and worthwhile. This, it is claimed, is the genuine way to raise standards. Mandatory testing aims to raise standards indirectly through the pressure of accountability, but any rise in average test score may reflect only a spurious improvement in test-taking skills. Authentic assessment aims to raise standards directly by improving teaching and learning, relating testing closely to instruction so that its influence in the classroom will (hopefully) be beneficial.

"Alternative assessment" is sometimes used to include modifications to conventional testing described above (level 2); but usually it implies a more radical departure from conventional testing. Dwyer (1990) writes of "a fundamental paradigm shift from an emphasis on prediction and control to an emphasis on meaning and understanding"; and Wolf *et al.* (1991) state: "The design and implementation of these new forms of assessments will entail nothing less than a wholesale transition from what we call a 'testing culture' to an 'assessment culture'."

The boundary between radical reform and modifications is not firm: progressive minor changes are a necessary first step towards major changes of attitude. In its restricted meaning, alternative assessment includes portfolios, records of achievement and profiles, continuous assessment, and modules which include statements of objectives as "criteria for evaluation" (see Chapter 5). In its wider meaning, alternative assessment extends to self-assessment, the capacity to judge one's own standards of achievement and to use that judgement diagnostically and formatively to promote further learning, as a prime aim of education. In particular, alternative assessment takes account of the affective element in learning: the importance of establishing an appropriate attitude or disposition to learning, and creating a supportive climate; and the key roles of relationships, self-image and perceptions of the task in learning. (These points are discussed more fully in Chapter 9.)

There are two main lines of criticism of this approach: the extra resources required, and its public credibility. Alternative assessment is not easy to implement. It makes a greater demand, not less, than conventional examining; and consequently it is more costly in its demands on time and the need for appropriate training, for both teachers and learners. Perhaps more important, it represents a paradigm shift which has not yet won acceptance even within the teaching profession or from parents and public. It does not readily answer the requirements for hard evidence on pupils' performance (though its evidence may in fact be more "valid"), or for comparability between schools, between teachers and between individual pupils. It shifts the locus of control, delegating much of this power to individual teachers and schools. There are problems in scoring, but the production of a score is not the main function of alternative assessment. Conventional testing is judged in terms of validity and reliability, but these terms require redefinition if they are to be applied to alternative assessment (see Chapter 8): for example, it is argued, the validity of a measure should be judged in terms of its effect on learning, how far it fosters development of the knowledge and skills specified in curricular objectives. Messick (1989) suggests the concept of "consequential validity" to refer to the impact of a test on classroom teaching.

Issues

The authors of the country reports in the chapters which follow were asked to focus on the two key themes, national testing and new approaches to assessment, and to identify issues of concern. Their reports raise many practical issues in implementing assessment policies. Administrators tend to look to research to provide evidence on which to base decisions on these issues: the decisions which they seek are within the framework of their existing national policies, as is appropriate. An international review, however, reveals how different these national policies are, and necessarily raises wider issues.

These are underlying conflicts in our expectations of assessment. Current concern has its origins in public dissatisfaction with educational provision (leading to demands for national testing, teacher appraisal and greater parental involvement) and in professional criticism of traditional assessment procedures (arguing instead for closer integration of teaching and assessment and greater autonomy for teachers). These conflicting attitudes are not readily reconcilable.

Assessment serves two general functions which also are difficult to reconcile:

-- as a measure of performance, of individual learners, of schools and of the system as a whole (a function associated with certification, accountability and control); and

-- as a natural part of the learning process (through feedback, guidance, diagnosis of difficulties, setting targets and motivation).

In the first of these functions, assessment can be seen as essentially external, in that there is measurement against criteria which are separate from the learning process. This mode of assessment is usually norm-referenced, and often takes the form of grades or test scores or ranking. For the second, assessment can be seen as essentially internal, in that the outcome is of value only so far as it is accepted by the learner: it is usually criterion-referenced, and the emphasis is on mastery of the content of learning. Conflict between these two functions is one source of dilemma in deciding the place and form of assessment in our education systems.

One crucial factor is not the nature of the tests themselves, but what depends on the results of the tests, "high stakes" or "low". Thus it is the place of assessment in the education system as a whole which is the focus of concern, and not just the particular content or style of testing. The important issues in assessment are not of technique but of policy: less a question of finding an ideal form of testing but rather of deciding how the results should be used. Of course, these two aspects are interdependent: form may determine or limit use.

There is potential conflict also between the implicit models underlying different approaches to assessment. The objectives model currently favoured in educational planning identifies targets of attainment which are prescribed for pupils and teachers. The model of constructivist learning theory which has developed strongly in the past 20 years emphasizes the importance of building on aspirations with which learners themselves identify. If the question is one of responsibility -- who ultimately is responsible for deciding the content and coverage of the curriculum, the State, the teachers or the learners themselves? -- then one may reasonably answer that it is a shared responsibility and that ideally each should act in a way to support the actions of the others.

The 1990 Annual Report of the Educational Testing Service in the United States optimistically detects

> "some consensus within what might be called 'the educational testing reform movement' as to the general directions testing needs to go if educational objectives are to be realised." (ETS, 1990)

This consensus accepts the "instructional" function of assessment as paramount; and hopefully the view is not confined to the testing reform movement. The view is summarised by Hargreaves (1989) in describing assessment "as part of learning, rather than a judgment passed on performance once the learning is over".

It is expressed more fully by Glaser (1990) in the concept of "assessment as enablement":

> "To place tests in the service of learning, we must foster an environment in which tests are seen as measures of those forms of human competence that are essential to future learning rather than merely as indices to current or past achievement. Once mastered, the skills and knowledge of a domain should be viewed as enabling competences for the future ... This attitude of enablement motivates us to assess knowledge in terms of its constructive use for future action. Our tests should ask: Can students use their current achievement to gather further information, evaluate evidence, enact as aesthetic performance, weigh alternative courses of action, and articulate reasoned arguments and decisions?"

REFERENCES

BROADFOOT,P. (1990), Personal communication.

CROOKS, T. J. (1988), "The impact of classroom evaluation practices on students", *Review of Educational Research*, 58 (4), 438-481.

DWYER, C. A. (1990), "Trends in the assessment of teaching and learning: Educational and methodological perspectives", in Broadfoot, P., Murphy, R. and Torrance, H. (eds.) *Changing Educational Assessment: International perspectives and trends.* London: Routledge.

EDUCATIONAL TESTING SERVICE (1990), *Helping America Raise Educational Standards for the 21st Century: 1990 Annual Report.* Princeton: ETS.

GLASER, R. (1990), "Toward new models for assessment", *International Journal of Educational Research*, 14 (5), 475-483.

HARGREAVES, A. (1989), *Curriculum and Assessment Reform.* Milton Keynes: Open University Press.

MESSICK, S. (1989), "Validity", in Linn, R. L. (ed.), *Educational measurement* (3rd edition). New York: Macmillan.

MURPHY, J. (ed.) (1990), *The Educational Reform Movement of the 1980s.* Berkeley: McCutchan.

STAKE, R. (1990), Personal communication.

WOLF, D., BIXBY, J., GLEEN, J. III and GARDNER, H. (1991), "To use their minds well: Investigating new forms of student assessment", *Review of Research in Education*, 17, 31-74.

Chapter 2

FRANCE

by
Professor Patricia Broadfoot
University of Bristol

The context for change

In 1984 three million people engaged in demonstrations on the streets of Paris in protest against proposed educational reforms. In 1986, further demonstrations by *lycée* and university students were the response to Mr. Monory's attempts to reform the *baccalauréat* examination and entry procedures for higher education. In 1990 *lycée* students again engaged in massive demonstrations against the quality of conditions in schools -- particularly in the *lycées*. This is because, in common with many other countries, France is seeking to face up to the challenge of providing education and training of an appropriate kind and level which will ensure a sufficient pool of skilled labour to meet the needs of industry in the future. As well as the massive expansion of provision at all levels, this goal also requires a movement away from the celebrated homogeneity and central control of French education in favour of a measure of decentralisation and institutional autonomy to allow for greater flexibility of response to the very real different educational needs of students within the system. Current developments in educational assessment are readily understood in terms of main themes: the need to make education more accessible to a wider range of students, and the need to reassure the public that quality and national equality are being maintained as the accepted pattern of national direction, monitoring and control gives way to greater local variation.

The French education system

Figure 1 sets out in tabular form the current structure of the French education system. The recently reformed structure now involves five years in the elementary school, followed by a common first two years in the comprehensive *collège*. Progress during this observational cycle is evaluated by a range of teachers and other professionals, who in discussion with parents decide the options for the *quatrième* and *troisième* (ages 14-16) -- most often the continuation of a general curriculum in the "orientation" cycle. For those who wish to move more rapidly into vocational training there is the option of a preparatory fourth year as the first of a three-year course in a *Lycée Professionnel*. Further options include *classes professionnelles de niveau* which provide a remedial option for students with difficulties and *classes préparatoires à l'apprentissage* which lead more directly to an apprenticeship. At the end of the third year students can choose between general or

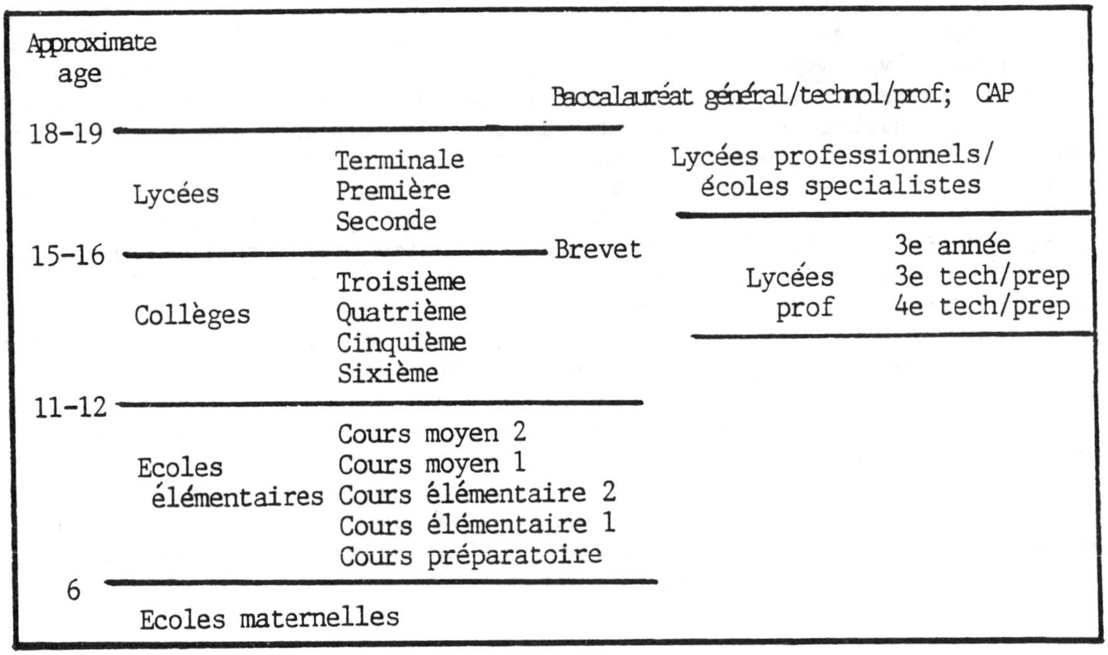

```
Approximate
   age
                                        Baccalauréat général/technol/prof;  CAP
 18-19
                       Terminale       Lycées professionnels/
           Lycées      Première        écoles specialistes
                       Seconde
 15-16                                 ──── Brevet                 3e année
                       Troisième            Lycées      3e tech/prep
           Collèges    Quatrième            prof        4e tech/prep
                       Cinquième
                       Sixième
 11-12
                       Cours moyen 2
           Ecoles      Cours moyen 1
           élémentaires Cours élémentaire 2
                       Cours élémentaire 1
                       Cours préparatoire
   6
           Ecoles maternelles
```

Figure 1. The education system to age 18/19 in France, 1991 (simplified and adapted from the Office National d'Information sur les Enseignements et les Professions, ONISEP)

technological studies in the *lycée* or a chosen vocational study at a *lycée professionnel*.

Assessment is important at various stages in the French education system. A range of qualifications provides each of these options with a recognised diploma at the end, as Figure 1 indicates. Having taken the *diplôme national du brevet* at the end of 3e (age 16), students will continue either towards the *baccalauréat général* or *technologique*, which is the passport to higher education. Alternatively, they may continue in a professional lycée to undertake a two-year course culminating in a *certificat d'aptitude professionnelle* (CAP) or a *brevet d'études professionnelles* (BEP). *Lycées professionnels* also offer the option of a *baccalauréat professionnel*. This range of qualifications, many of which, like the *baccalauréat technologique*, are innovations, reflects the attempts that have been made in recent years to retain more young people for longer in the education system and to put more emphasis on the generation of high-level vocational and technological skill. The clearest illustration of this policy is the commitment by President Mitterrand, who has made education the major theme of his second term of office, to getting 80 per cent of the year group achieving a pass in the *baccalauréat* examination or its equivalent by the year 2000, in contrast to the mere 15 per cent who achieved this goal during the 1960s (Ministère de l'Education nationale, 1989).

But the rapid expansion of the system has also caused many strains to be apparent, manifested in increasing class sizes, increases in the student/teacher ratio to the level of one of the highest among OECD countries and a steady deterioration in the provision and quality of school buildings. Coupled with this is the inability of the system to cope with the diverse needs of the students it now contains, and in particular the 100 000 students who, every year, leave without any formal certificate. The espoused aims of French educational policy now embrace the need to modernise the curriculum in line with changes in the nature of knowledge and the way it is to be applied, including in particular the promotion of more inter-disciplinary and general studies, the promotion of more individualised teaching, the creation of provision for on-going appraisal and guidance for students, and the encouragement of a much greater degree of teamwork among teachers.

Unfortunately the attitudes of both teachers and parents have not been so quick to change. The combination of a "massification" of the education system and the new problems that the retention of a wider social range of students post-16 has brought with it, plus the increasing variety of provision, has led to massive public disquiet about apparently falling standards. Despite the evidence of careful research such as that of Establet and Baudelot in their book, *Le Niveau Monte*, which shows standards to be in fact rising, a sustained press campaign, coupled with lack of public esteem for teachers, continues to fuel widespread anxiety. Public conservatism is matched by the "*fort esprit de conservatisme*" (quotation from interview) among teachers -- especially those of highest status in the *lycées* who, through their unions, resist repeated attempts to change both the structure of and the approach to schooling. Successive ministers of education -- both left and right wing -- have tried to reform both the *lycée* and its flagship, the *baccalauréat* examination, but in each case the powerful subject lobbies have combined with the teacher unions to resist change.

The need for radical change in the education system and the need to reassure public opinion about the maintenance of standards if such attempts at change are to have any chance of successful realisation provide a framework for interpreting recent developments in assessment in France. In what follows, two themes are identified as characterising the major elements in such development: (1) the national monitoring of standards of student achievement and mechanisms for promoting institutional quality control, and (2) the development of more curriculum-integrated approaches to assessment which provide for the growing diversity of both student needs and learning outcomes.

1. Standards and national testing

The increasing heterogeneity of French educational provision brought about by the attempts to introduce a measure of decentralisation in recent decades, plus the rapid expansion of student numbers in the post-compulsory sector, have prompted the central administration to institute national monitoring of educational standards to ensure that "value for money" is being provided. Whereas in France central control of the various inputs into the education system has traditionally been regarded as a sufficient basis for accountability (see Broadfoot, 1983), policy-makers now appear to feel the need both for more explicit mechanisms of quality control and for better information on which to base policy decisions at all levels of the system from individual schools to central ministry.

National monitoring

Thus in 1974 the then Minister of Education M. Fontanet set up a national programme for evaluating student results "to gather, analyse and to put at the disposition of the Minister the information necessary to evaluate in their various aspects the results of education and training activities and their longer-term evolution" (Circular 74-204, 1974). All relevant parties in the education system -- inspectors, teachers, school principals, researchers, administrators and technicians -- were involved in the working group charged with designing the surveys which have taken place at regular intervals (at least once every five years) and cover the full range of knowledge, skills, behaviour and opinions across the curriculum. Five surveys have taken place at primary school level since 1979, four at *collège* since 1982 and four at *lycée* level since 1985 which have covered all the year groups in rotation.

The year groups which have been tested (Ministère de l'Education nationale, 1990a) are:

In primary school: *cours préparatoire* (7 year-olds) 1979; *cours élémentaire 2* (9 year-olds) 1981, 1989/90 assessment of the whole age cohort; *cours moyen 1* (10 year-olds) 1981; *cours moyen 2* (11 year-olds) 1983-1987; **in collège**: 6e 1989, 1989/90 whole age cohort assessment; 5e 1982-1988; 3e 1984-1990; **in lycée**: *seconde* 1986; *première* 1987 (French); *terminale-baccalauréat*, history + geography 1987, English 1988.

Using mainly a mixture of multiple choice and structured written questions, surveys are carried out on a sample of schools chosen to reflect differences in size, type and rural/urban location. For each subject, the test takes about one hour and the total may amount to about one week per student. The tests are administered in carefully controlled conditions and marked by teachers according to strict guidelines to ensure comparability. Recently attempts have been made to include less objective assessment techniques including oral assessment of verbal expression in a foreign language and observation, for example, in the evaluation of creativity in body language. Attempts are also being made to assess cross-curricular skills.

By re-using certain tests these surveys provide some comparison of standards over time, although this is problematic where the context of the curriculum has changed. The surveys also provide the necessary data base for the increasingly felt need for international comparisons of standards. Thirdly the survey results are designed to identify particular patterns of error and relate particular factors in the education system concerning, for example, teaching approach and student background, to results. Thus, the information is seen as providing an important aid to policy-making.

Assessment of student learning outcomes at the end of learning cycles: Opération CE2/6e

Since 1989, these monitoring surveys have been complemented by an annual comprehensive evaluation in both state and private schools of the attainments in French and maths of all students in CE2 (third year of primary school) and *sixième* (first year of college) (1.7 million students). This important initiative is conducted in the second week of the school year in order to provide teachers as they begin work with their class with a detailed diagnostic picture of the strengths and weaknesses of individual children so that the teacher can respond differentially to each child's needs. The aim is to encourage a more individualised pedagogy and by so doing, to improve the overall level of student learning given the significant numbers of students experiencing difficulties in basic skills on entry to *collège* which was identified by previous national monitoring.

Once again, this initiative is a reflection both of the increasing diversity of students need and the general lack of tradition or training among French teachers in coping with such diversity. An important part of the initiative involves the provision of training courses in assessment run by national and local inspectors for teachers. Although the assessment instruments have so far been devised nationally, the longer-term aim is for more local provision to become the norm, tailored to local conditions and needs. Crucially it is hoped that in time teachers can be provided -- or indeed provide themselves -- with assessment materials that, with training, they will be willing and able to use as an integral part of their teaching, in order better to provide for diagnosing and responding to individual students' needs.

The evaluation is based on four 25-minute tests in maths and French and takes about four days to complete. The results of the largely written tests are marked according to standardized coding guidelines so that teachers can analyse class results, for which purpose they are provided with a software package.

Information about their child's performance is given to parents, and many schools are setting aside time for discussion of results with parents.

The unprecedentedly high level of parent interest and response provoked by the evaluation is regarded as one of the major achievements of the initiative providing, as it does, both for the kind of constructive, close dialogue between schools and families which has not hitherto been a feature of French education and for a measure of direct accountability to parents concerning standards.

If the aim of improving student learning through nationally initiated formative assessment also embraces training teachers in assessment and helping them to devise ways of responding to student need in a "regular and rigorous manner", an associated aim is to encourage a school-wide response to this need. Although the main role of these assessments is officially at least to provide formative information for teachers and to encourage and equip them to be better formative assessors themselves, the programme also has an important summative dimension in that aggregated results are published nationally so that parents, teachers and headteachers can compare their "results" against national norms.

Although the availability of such information has provoked considerable media interest nationally, the Ministry has so far resisted pressure for results to be made public and thus to provide for inter-school or inter-region comparisons. The still strongly-held French belief in the notion of equality and commonality in educational provision militates against the adoption of the notion of competition and market forces to stimulate efforts by individual schools to improve standards. The assumption is rather of a common problem which schools must be enabled to tackle. But, given the experiments with open enrolment currently taking place in Paris and the intense interest that the annual publication of *baccalauréat* results in *Le Monde de l'Education* provokes, it may not be long before the pressure for aggregated results to be published becomes irresistible -- at least on a regional basis.

Meanwhile, an increasing sense of local ownership in the conduct of the evaluations, combined with the relatively "low stakes" of an assessment that takes place at the beginning of the school year and is therefore not part of the "orientation" process, is leading to increasingly general support for the initiative. The initial reaction of teachers to the very rushed imposition of this initiative was predictably negative. The profession is accustomed to resisting change and to seeing assessment of this kind as external and imposed, is not committed to the concept of an individualised pedagogy and has little or no tradition of formative assessment. Teachers were suspicious that the aim was really to assess them rather than their students.

However, research studies (Ministère de l'Education nationale 1990b, 1991a; Gilles, 1990) report an increasingly favourable response among both teachers and parents to the tests themselves and the information produced. Teachers report considerable problems with organisation of training and much hostility has centred on the heavy load of recording which needs to be improved and simplified (Le Guen, 1991). Teachers feel they need more training and support to undertake the third element in the three-pronged strategy of information, training (formation) and remediation, and certainly evaluation of the initiative reveals that in only a very small number of cases was a learning remediation project even formulated within the school, let alone implemented (Gilles, 1990). A crucial aim for the future will be to encourage the formulation of the school-level policies, currently almost totally absent, which will be needed if there is to be effective integration of curriculum and assessment in terms of remediation.

At a press conference in April 1991, M. Jospin, then Minister of Education, announced the decision to implement a similar national evaluation in Autumn 1992 at the beginning of the first year of *lycée* studies *(seconde)*. This decision reflects the realisation now apparently common to many countries that even in a highly centralised system, it is still difficult and yet increasingly important really to know what students can do and how they learn.

Institutional evaluation

As the process of decentralisation has proceeded, the laws of 1983 and 1986 promoted the idea of the school as a local public establishment which, with the support in each *académie* of teams of trained teachers or consultants, must now develop a written and public plan against which the whole community can judge the institution's degree of success in meeting its own goals. An assumption, now enshrined in law, that individual schools might vary in their policies and that teachers should be accountable through their institutions rather than as individuals subject to personal inspection, represents a major change in French education. This change is reflected in the fact that the national inspectorate is also now responsible for evaluating institutions rather than as they were before, nominally at least, charged with inspecting individual teachers.

In 1989 the *Loi d'Orientation* laid down the procedures for evaluating schools. The school has to carry out a detailed self-evaluation as a preparatory study to an external inspection using a range of indicators and the results of both studies form the basis of subsequent discussion between school staff and inspector (CERI/OECD, 1990). Currently *collèges* are not using student results gathered for the orientation process as part of their public accountability profile although there is pressure on them to do so (Coqblin, 1991).

2. Developments in assessment techniques

This section reviews tensions and trends in the assessment and certification of student achievement in its three principal manifestations -- teacher assessment and reporting, the 16+ *brevet* examination and the 18+ *baccalauréat* examination.

Assessment by teachers

Assessment of pupil learning in France is frequent and formal. A recent survey by the National Inspectorate found that for formative assessment purposes the use of numerical marks is still totally dominant at every level -- as is the use of written exercises for assessment which take up, in *troisième* and *seconde*, up to 20 per cent of the timetable. In fact, such evaluation has, in practice, been largely summative with students receiving a mark *(contrôle)* every fortnight or month which goes into their cumulative record or *livret scolaire*. At the end of each term the *conseil de classe* meets to discuss each student's progress as the basis for a termly report *(bulletin)* and at the relevant career points, to decide their "orientation" for the future

(Broadfoot, 1984). Research by *Inspection Générale de l'Education nationale* (IGEN) reveals that each pupil receives between 30 seconds and 4 minutes of consideration and that of the total discussion, 50 per cent is devoted to giving general information about results, and 30 per cent is concerned with the behaviour and attitude to work of the students, meaning that less than 20 per cent of the discussion is devoted to considering how to help students make progress or to considering what would be the best orientation decision for each. Thus, although dialogue is increasingly being regarded as the keynote of student orientation so that orientation can become more continuous, educative and collaborative, its implementation in practice is slow. In addition to the usual barriers to change and the difficult challenge in the French context of achieving the necessary whole-school approach, Coqblin (1991) argues that this development is being hindered by the lack of a precise framework of achievement criteria. In the French context, the movement away from the language of marks in favour of the language of interpretation appears extremely subjective and open to differences in interpretation.

> "It thus appears that personal improvisation remains the norm for the assessment of students. Evaluation remains summative, institutionalised in the form of frequent written exercises without a sufficient degree of interest being taken in student progress nor in the identification of learning difficulties." (Bottin, 1991, p. 38)

Apart from the lack of genuinely formative assessment and guidance, a consideration of the pattern of teacher assessment reveals two further issues of importance. The first concerns the predominance of numerical marks despite widespread recognition that they are unconstructive and difficult to interpret (Bottin, 1991) because of the lack of explicit objectives and criteria. IGEN concludes that teachers need better tools if they are to get both the maximum benefit from their assessment efforts and be better able to tailor their teaching so that students understand the reasons for their success or failure. At present students tend to disregard the comments made by teachers about their work. To remedy this situation the Inspectors recommend that there should be an improvement in the precision of assessment objectives so that students, teachers and policy-makers can understand and use them, and an increase in the number and methods of assessment used.

The second, less obvious issue in this respect, centres on teachers' comments in the *livret scolaire* (Broadfoot, 1984) which also includes teachers' comments concerning application, discipline and the like. In the more highly selective parts of the French education system -- the prestigious *lycées* and the preparatory classes for the highly selective *Grandes Ecoles*, the *dossier* can play a role as important as the *baccalauréat* in determining who "fits" and who does not. This situation provides an important illustration of the tension between a system which has traditionally placed enormous emphasis on evaluation techniques (Dosnon, 1991) that are as objective and impersonal as possible -- as in the formal written examination -- and one that, as in the Bourdieu and Passeron (1977) document, places subtle but considerable emphasis on selecting as future members of the élite those students who demonstrate the right personal and social qualities or "cultural capital" in Bourdieu's terms.

The significance of the perceived personal and social dimension as part of the qualities of "the good pupil" explains much of the current tension in French education. The system has long been geared to delivering education to students with similar social and cultural values to those of the teachers; but now it is trying to respond adequately to the needs of a much wider range of students in an era when social and cultural norms are also changing rapidly. As teachers struggle to implement formative assessment which will help them respond to students' different needs, they are also struggling to overcome their suspicion of apparently less objective assessment techniques -- notably continuous assessment -- which are part of the current agenda for educational reform.

Le Diplôme National du Brevet

Since the abolition of the *brevet d'études du premier cycle* (BEPC) in 1980, several approaches to the certification of student achievement at the end of *collège* have been tried and the relevant qualification currently is the *diplôme national du brevet* (DNB). With the goal of 80 per cent of students studying for the *baccalauréat*, the DNB is not intended as a terminal assessment but a stage along the way. The DNB attests that students have achieved a certain standard in their studies. It acts as a challenge to motivate some pupils, and to give them their first experience of an examination. In the *collège* the result is based on an examination in French, maths, history and geography and on the results of continuous assessment. But whilst the locally-set examination is rigorously standardized, there is little or no moderation of the continuous assessment awarded by the school, which tends to be over-generous in its marking. Even so, in many places the percentage of students achieving average marks is too low so that the whole distribution is moderated up to ensure 20 per cent of candidates achieve an acceptable standard. This results in inequalities between different *départements* and penalisation of the more rigorous, leading to widespread doubts about the value of the results.

An apparently more useful way forward is being pioneered in the academy of Lille which is using a detailed marking and reporting system to provide diagnostic feedback for teachers (Caroff, 1991).

The baccalauréat

It is widely recognised among policy-makers that the *baccalauréat* needs changing (Ministère de l'Education nationale, 1991b). It takes too long out of the school year and dominates the curriculum. The problem of the arbitrary domination of maths and science specialisms in the *baccalauréat* has long been a source of concern since it means students choose their specialisms, notably maths, on the basis of that subject's ranking in the pecking order rather than its relevance to their needs.

Practical problems also dictate the need for change including a shortage of markers for the huge numbers of scripts now being generated. Whilst the shortcomings of the overcrowded and impersonal *lycée* are overcome for those with the means to buy the provision of private tuition, the large number of families without such a recourse continues to fuel the pressure for teachers to update their teaching approach from lecturing to facilitating the learning of their students. Jospin's April 1991 initiative "for the reform of the *lycée*" which provides, among other things, for students to have three hours a week in their principal subjects for more individual work, including any particular help they may need, gives emphasis to the perceived need for students to become more active learners and, in consequence, for teachers to change their teaching approach.

Given the dominating influence of the *baccalauréat* on the teaching style, subject matter and the kinds of learning outcome sought in the *lycée* and even, to an extent, in the *collège* (Huissenet, 1991), the Ministry is seeking to introduce change via provision for continuous assessment -- currently being used in both the 16+ *brevet* and the more vocational *baccalauréat professionnel* taught in the *lycées professionnels* (LEP).

In these latter institutions, experimentation with the use of continuous assessment has been going on for fifteen years. This has involved abandoning final examinations and marks and the introduction of teaching based on detailed course objectives with evaluation checklists comprising detailed and precise criteria. Courses are modularised and there is some student self-assessment.

Teachers of the BEP and the CAP in the LEP, however, complain that the continuing formality of their role and the return to the use of marks militate against the spirit of continuous assessment; also that the time needed for it is not recognised. Consequently, there is now a decline in the use of continuous assessment. In relation to vocational training courses, 80 per cent of senior staff support continuous assessment as providing for both more valid assessment and student-centred pedagogy as well as avoiding the end-of-year chaos. However, many teachers fear being vulnerable to outside pressures and of being accused of favouritism, and they also doubt the national value of a qualification in which teachers have a say in the results of their own students.

Given the very strong support for the *baccalauréat* as an anonymous, external examination among students, parents and teachers and as a guarantee of equality against the influence of teachers' values and schools of different status, all attempts at reforming the *bac* have so far largely failed. The baccalauréat is a *"rite de passage"* -- any reform that does not maintain its ritual status appears devaluing.

The recommendation of the *Conseil national des Programmes sur l'Evolution du Lycée* is for modes of assessment to be chosen according to the purpose of the assessment and the competences to be assessed. They recommend therefore that all diplomas should be a mixture of national, anonymous tests and continuous assessment, the balance between the two being determined as appropriate. It nevertheless remains to be seen if Jospin's June 1991 initiative to introduce continuous assessment and access to university without necessarily having the *bac* will succeed where other such attempts have failed.

Commentary

Among the various purposes fulfilled by assessment, it is possible to distinguish three main groups -- formative, summative and evaluative. Among the first might be included diagnostic assessment and assessment undertaken to encourage the right learning attitudes and styles (Crooks, 1989); among the second would be included both the attestation of competence and selection; among the third would figure the various dimensions of accountability, performance indicators and quality control. Although all these purposes may be argued to be legitimate applications of assessment procedures, it is rare that the same procedures will adequately meet all three main purposes simultaneously. The detailed, frequent, positive and idiosyncratic feedback associated with good formative assessment would be inappropriate as the basis either for institutional monitoring or summative certification. The design of a criterion-referenced test for determining competence will seek to maximise success whereas that designed for selection must spread the distribution of scores as widely as possible.

In considering recent developments in assessment in French education, it is apparent that only one of the three broad purposes identified above -- the summative -- has traditionally been in evidence. Thus, whilst considerable attention has always been given to marking students' work for the summative purposes of reports and examinations, very little use appears to have been made of assessment as a device to support learning. Equally, the same rigorous summative assessment appears to have provided sufficient reassurance as to standards that it has itself operated as a form of quality control.

This review has identified some of the very profound social pressures which have led to the beginnings of significant change in the traditional emphasis of assessment purposes. In France, as in other countries, the overriding educational priority is now to boost the overall level of educational achievement within the population as a whole. International developments in assessment techniques such as the growing dominance of criterion-referenced approaches, more authentic measures of achievement, and more democratic, participatory assessment practices appear to have convinced policy-makers in France, as elsewhere, of the potentially key role assessment can play as part of the teaching-learning process itself. Equally, policy-makers appear to have been convinced both of the similarly formative role assessment can play at the institutional level and of the need to protect the scope for implementing such techniques by ensuring that the inevitable anxiety provoked by change is adequately addressed by the provision of comprehensive reassurance that the standards agenda is not simultaneously being abandoned.

While this change of emphasis from summative to formative assessment is a common feature of societies where the educational priority has swung from that of weeding students out of education, in favour of keeping students in education, France presents what is arguably a unique context for realising this potential of assessment given that there is both a deep-rooted commitment to national, summative examinations and little tradition of concern with the technique, rather than the content of teaching. The long-standing ideological commitment to national unity and equality which has shaped French educational attitudes in the past still produces powerful resistance to any attempt to alter anything that might diminish that unity. As a result, externally-conducted examinations tend to carry a significance that does not extend to curriculum-integrated assessment. Furthermore, the lack of a strong pedagogic tradition, even in primary schools, reflects a perspective in which subject expertise, rather than teaching technique, defines the teacher's professional identity. Thus, as well as training teachers in how to do assessment -- an omission from initial training that has been well nigh universal until recently -- in France it is also necessary to change many teachers' perspective of what it is to teach before any such training can begin to take place profitably.

Finally, the traditionally highly centralised administration of French education has not tended to foster enthusiasm for grass-roots developments. Although experiments with new ideas are a consistent feature of French education, these are not typically initiated by teachers themselves. The lack of a tradition of institutional autonomy has tended further to inhibit locally-initiated developments. Thus, new ideas concerning assessment practices must still be both generated and implemented from the centre which, by definition, tends to result in over-generalisation of strategies which cannot be either an integral part of curriculum planning or reflect institutional circumstances and local needs. In short, teachers have few models of the potential of formative assessment techniques being successfully realised to act as a spur to change.

But if the tradition of equality, and hence of the need for central direction of curricula and resources, inhibits the development of new, more formative assessment techniques, it also provides one of the most interesting contrasts to the implementation of "high stakes" testing currently characteristic of many anglophone countries. The implementation of comprehensive monitoring of national standards at certain "key stages" which is explicitly designed not to provide comparative teacher and institutional data offers an important opportunity to gauge the impact of monitoring which is much more formative in its inspiration. The timing of the assessment at the beginning of the school year and the fact that results are confidential to schools and teachers, show a genuine attempt on the part of policy-makers to resist the pressure that undoubtedly exists for assessment to become the currency of an educational market-place. Whilst, as in many other countries, the manipulation of assessment practices in France is becoming an increasingly important policy tool, it appears to be a tool that is being manipulated primarily with a view to putting more, rather than less, emphasis on the professional skills of teachers. This is in contrast to countries such as the United Kingdom where failure adequately to provide for public reassurance over standards in recent years has resulted in a backlash of increasing central control at the expense of trust in teacher professionalism.

It remains to be seen, however, how long central government will be able to pursue its reform agenda of establishing assessment as part of the language of curriculum in the face of entrenched public and professional conservatism which sees assessment largely in summative terms, and the seductive attractions of a market model, based on an evaluative role for assessment, which is already manifest in some of the big cities where limited experiments in providing more parental choice through open enrolment are being conducted.

Acknowledgements

The assistance of the following is gratefully acknowledged: colleagues from the Ministry of Education, Youth and Sports, especially André Huissenet, Thierry Soupault, Martine Le Guen, Pierre Garrigue, Anne Corbett, Mary Follain, Isabelle Delfau and Norberto Bottani.

REFERENCES

BOTTIN, J. (1991), "Etude des pratiques d'évaluation des professeurs en classes de troisième et de seconde", *Rapport sur l'Inspection générale de l'Education nationale,* Paris.

BOURDIEU, P. and PASSERON, J. P. (1977), *Reproduction.* London: Sage.

BROADFOOT, P. M. (1983), "Assessment constraints on curriculum practice: a comparative study", in Hammersley, M. and Hargreaves, A. (eds) *Curriculum Practice: Some sociological case studies.* Lewes: Falmer Press.

BROADFOOT, P. M. (1984), "From public examinations to profile assessment: the case of France", in Broadfoot, P. M. (ed), *Selection, Certification and Control.* Lewes: Falmer.

CAROFF, A. (1991), "Evaluation et validation des acquis: le diplôme national du brevet", in Ministère de l'Education nationale de la Jeunesse et des Sports, *Rapport sur l'Evaluation des Acquis des Elèves à la fin des Cycles d'Apprentissage,* Paris.

CERI/OECD (1990), *"The Role of Central Inspectorates in the Assessment of Schools: Report on France."* OECD Conference, Strasbourg. Paris: OECD.

CIRCULAR No. 74-204 (24.5.1974), "Sur les missions et attributions du service d'informations économiques et statistiques", Paris: Ministère de l'Education nationale, de la Jeunesse et des Sports.

COQBLIN, A. (1991), "La politique d'orientation des collèges", *in* Ministère de l'Education nationale, de la Jeunesse et des Sports, *Rapport sur l'Evaluation des Acquis des Elèves à la fin des Cycles d'Apprentissage,* Paris.

CROOKS, T. (1989), "Impact of classroom evaluation practices on students", *Review of Educational Research,* 58, 438-481.

DOSNON, O. (1991), *Les Recherches sur l'Evaluation à l'INETOP.* Paris: Service de Recherches de l'INETOP.

GILLES, M. and associates (1990), "Bilan diagnostic des effets, chez les enseignants, de l'opération évaluation-formation CE2-6e". Paris.

HUISSENET, A. (1991), *Propositions du Conseil national des Programmes sur l'Evolution du Lycée: Second Rapport.* Paris: Ministère de l'Education nationale, de la Jeunesse et des Sports.

LE GUEN, M. (1991), *L'Evaluation de l'Acquis des Elèves: Direction de l'évaluation et de la prospective*. Paris: Ministère de l'Education nationale, de la Jeunesse et des Sports.

MINISTÈRE DE L'EDUCATION NATIONALE, DE LA JEUNESSE ET DES SPORTS (1989) *Educational Evaluation and Reform Strategies: National policies and strategies*. Paris: OECD.

---- (1990a) Response to OECD national survey.

---- (1990b) Evaluation CE2-6e: Résultats nationaux septembre 1989.

---- (1991a) Evaluation CE2-6e: Résultats nationaux septembre 1990.

---- (1991b) Conférence de presse: "Propositions pour la rénovation du lycée" (22.4.1991).

Chapter 3

GERMANY

by
Professor Margaret Sutherland
University of Leeds

Assessment procedures in Germany are remarkable for relying greatly on the ability of individual teachers to use their professional judgement. At all levels of the school system it is the assessment made by teachers using a simple, traditional marking scale that counts. Assessment follows the curriculum and is clearly related to it. At the same time, there is a high degree of teacher accountability to education authorities, to pupils and to parents.

National standards

Analysis of assessment and its importance in the schools of Germany is complicated by the fact that each of the states (Länder) is free to determine its own education system. In the post-war era, West Germany reverted to the traditional *Kulturhoheit* (educational and cultural autonomy) of its eleven states. Each state has its own Ministry of Education and its own legislation determining the administration and provision of education: hence, each state has its own school structures, its own arrangements for assessment, its prescriptions for curriculum content. Since the five states formerly constituting the German Democratic Republic are at present in a transition period, moving from a firmly centralised system towards the same kind of organisation as prevailed in the Federal Republic of Germany, the following discussion is based on the situation in the eleven "West German" states. Although the former "East German" states are, since 1990, also entitled to *Kulturhoheit*, it remains to be seen how they may develop individual systems while at the same time honouring undertakings to assimilate their provision of education to the situation already existing in West Germany.

Despite determined maintenance of individual autonomy, important general characteristics are common to the eleven Länder. Since the 1960s, a number of federal bodies have produced recommendations for reforming education and for harmonizing the provision made in different parts of the country. In particular, the deliberations of the *Kulturministerkonferenz* (KMK), the standing conference of the Ministers of Education, have produced agreements subsequently implemented by appropriate legislation within the individual Länder - though the implementation process allows some variation in interpretation. Most notably the KMK has produced agreements to ensure common conditions in the structure, conduct and subject composition of the *Abitur* examination at the end of full secondary schooling. Similar agreements have determined the subjects, optional and compulsory, to be studied at primary and lower secondary level and approximately the amount of time to be devoted to these subjects.

Some progress has thus been made towards ensuring equal opportunities in education: major qualifications obtained in different Länder are accepted as equivalent throughout the country. But each Land still determines the curriculum within its own schools and within subjects by publishing statements of what is to be taught at different levels. These statements have evolved from very detailed prescriptions of the content of each subject to more general indications of aims, subject content, methods and assessment, which yet leave some flexibility in application within schools. Such statements are usually produced on the basis of discussions between administrators and experienced teachers. Even so, Länder still differ in the degree of prescriptiveness of their *Richtlinien* (guidelines) or *lehrpläne* (teaching plans). Notable differences also remain in the differentiated provision of secondary education and in types of vocational education. These differences inevitably tend to be affected by the views of the political party in power within each Land, especially by long-established "progressive" or "conservative" Land governments.

It is therefore not possible to refer to attempts to assess national standards in German education: the relatively recent *Abitur* reforms by KMK agreement have perhaps come closest to establishing common practices, though not to assessing levels of success in achieving the goals set. It is for individual Länder to consider how effectively their system is working, though the annual federal publication of educational statistics does give information which could be the basis of interesting comparisons. Assessment procedures at present have mainly the function of deciding individuals' progress to the next stage of education: they are used for selection or certification rather than for creating or establishing norms.

One result of differences in the structure of school systems is that assessment becomes important for individual children at different points in their school career, according to the Land in which they are living. School education is compulsory throughout Germany from the age of 6: it may be completed after nine or ten years (according to the Land) but those who leave at this point must continue in vocational education (part-time or full-time) for two or three years. Within this framework, there has been much controversy about the length of primary education and the structure of the first years of secondary education. In West Berlin pupils remain in the common primary school for six years; in other Länder primary education lasts for only four years. Years 5 and 6 are, by federal agreement, an "orientation stage" during which children's varying abilities should be assessed so that they can go on to appropriate kinds of education; but in a few Länder this "orientation stage" is in separate schools while in others years 5 and 6 are part of differentiated secondary schools. Where years 5 and 6 are to be spent in differentiated schools, assessment at the end of year 4 (about age 10) is a matter likely to determine individuals' whole subsequent education, even if the system is theoretically open, allowing transfer to other schools later.

Assessment for selection

In all states, three types of secondary school are provided (see Figure 2):

- the *Hauptschule*, normally from year 5 (age 10-11) to year 9 or 10 (about age 16), receiving pupils likely to leave then for employment and/or vocational education;

- the *Realschule*, taking school years 5 to 10, offering general education at a higher level than that of the *Hauptschule* - this school has enjoyed increasing popularity in recent years;

- the *Gymnasium*, the academic secondary school, taking pupils from school year 5 to year 13, and concluding with the examination for the *Abitur* leaving certificate which gives the right to study at university.

There are also some comprehensive schools of different types, but such schools provide for only a small minority of the school population, though some states have developed them more extensively than others.

Assessment at the end of year 4 (about age 10), as at other educational levels, is expressed by the traditional mark scale which ranges from 1 to 6. The highest mark is 1, indicating work which is very good, well above average; 2 is good, fully up to standard; 3 is satisfactory, on the whole up to standard; 4 is adequate, passable; 5 is poor, defective; 6 is unsatisfactory, very poor. Thus 5 and 6 are fail marks: 5 indicates that the situation may perhaps be saved by further work, 6 is irretrievable failure. This scale, through constant use, is understood by all, in school and out of it. But giving marks of this kind has recently been abolished in year 1 of the primary school: and in year 2 such marks may be given for core subjects only or are still not used at all. Thus, to take the example of the process in North-Rhine-Westphalia, the primary class teacher writes on each pupil's record/report card, at half-yearly intervals, an indication of the pupil's progress in reading, arithmetic and writing as well as descriptive comments on the pupil's attitudes to learning and to interaction with others. This card is signed by the teacher and by the parent (or other person responsible for the child's education). From year 3 onwards, half-yearly marks are given for all subjects of the curriculum -- religious education (where applicable); speech; reading; writing; arithmetic; maths; introduction to environmental and other sciences; sport; music; art/textile work. The teacher also continues to supply descriptive comments on the child's attitudes, adjustment to work and to other people. Similarly in year 4, marks and comments on the pupil's performance are recorded.

As a result of this continuous observation, and in consultation with other teachers of the class, at the end of year 4 the class teacher signs a *Gutachten* (judgement/assessment) which sets out observations of the child's work in school and learning abilities -- understanding of tasks, ability to concentrate, independence -- and the conclusion as to whether the child is a) suited to *Gymnasium* or *Realschule*; b) perhaps suited to *Gymnasium* or *Realschule*; or c) not suited to *Gymnasium* or *Realschule*. If the child is

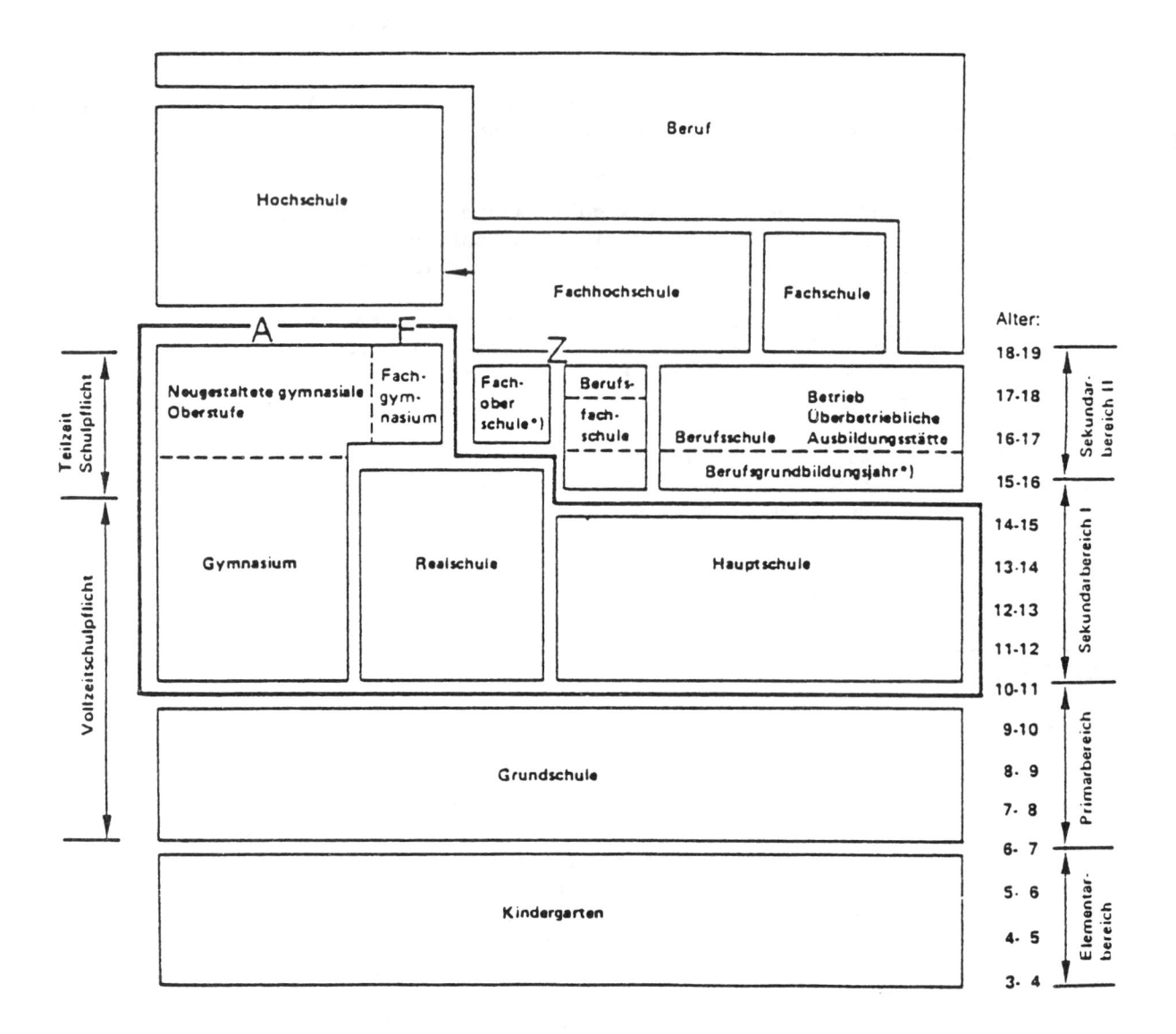

A: allgemeine Hochschulreife   F: fachgebundene Hochschulreife   Z: Fachhochschulreife

Figure 2. The education system of the Federal Republic of Germany, 1990 (from J. Kraus, *Schule und Lehrerberuf*, Deutscher Lehrerverband)

given assessment a) or b), the parent then applies to the preferred school and the school decides, on the basis of the *Gutachten*, whether to accept the child. (Falling numbers of children in recent years have increased schools' readiness to accept, indeed actively to recruit, more pupils.)

The child coming into category c) should enter a *Hauptschule*, or *Gesamtschule* (comprehensive) if the latter is available, though some comprehensives may be selective in their intake in order to maintain an acceptable balance of ability levels. But since the 1960s, the attitudes of many parents have changed so that where formerly some parents would accept the child's allocation to the *Hauptschule* contentedly (thinking the *Gymnasium* "not for the likes of us", campaigns were indeed mounted by educators to change such views. Now there is more widespread ambition to secure a "good" education for children and the more academic schools are seen as offering better chances in life. So some parents may challenge the assessment of their child as not suited to *Gymnasium* or *Realschule*.

In such cases a different assessment process comes into play. The child is assessed by *Probeunterricht* (probationary teaching, or testing through teaching). During three days the child, as part of a group of children in the same situation, is taught lessons and given tests by teachers who alternate in observing the child's responses to the work situations. As a result of this process, the group of teachers in question produces a second assessment. If the child is still judged "unsuitable for *Gymnasium* or *Realschule*", counselling is offered to the parents.

While the *Probeunterricht* might seem a realistic and fair form of assessment, it is criticised by many educators. The child is, they point out, in an unhappy situation, feeling already classified as a failure, being taught by unknown teachers in an unfamiliar setting. All this may conceal the child's full potential. On the other hand, the teaching-observing team, aware of all the factors involved, may tend to play it safe and give the verdict (b) (perhaps suitable), however poorly the child performs.

Details of such procedures may vary in different Länder: it also depends on the Land whether ultimately the parents are allowed to overrule the primary school's assessment -- Hessen, for example, does allow this. The advantages of such flexibility are recognised: teachers relieved of the "power of life or death" concerning the child's future schooling can serve as counsellors to parents, offering the results of school observations, explaining possibilities. Teacher in-service education in some cases is already trying to foster in teachers such counselling abilities, making them more aware of parents' susceptibilities and encouraging them to avoid confrontations.

It is further recognised in some Länder that a great deal of stress is created by the knowledge that the primary school child's performance in ordinary class work may determine the child's chances of academic secondary education, since it will affect the teacher's formal assessments. Parents consequently may worry considerably about primary school reports, and the child in turn may become worried and anxious. Another source of anxiety about school marks at all levels is that pupils not reaching a pass mark may be required to repeat the year.

In the "orientation stage" itself, in years 5 and 6, a kind of continuous assessment for educational guidance takes place. Class tests in the core subjects are given regularly and teachers meet at intervals during the year to discuss pupils' progress: towards the end of orientation years they can thus come to a decision as to what academic characteristics each pupil has and which type of secondary schooling seems suitable. But the importance of such decisions again depends on the Land's school policies. If the orientation stage takes place in free-standing institutions consisting only of classes 5 and 6, movement to the following school is straightforward enough. Where pupils are already in differentiated schools, transfers to a different type of school may be made but seem to be relatively infrequent.

Assessment for certification

School-leaving certificates

Transfers at later stages in secondary education depend on gaining appropriate leaving certificates -- or completion-of-course certificates -- at the end of year 9 (of the *Hauptschule*) or at the end of year 10 *(Hauptschule* or *Realschule).* (Pupils leaving the *Gymnasium* at the end of year 10 may similarly obtain a certificate that they have completed year 10 successfully.) Such certificates are important in gaining access, if the mark level is good enough, to higher forms of secondary education (especially to years 11-13 of the *Gymnasium*) or to higher levels of vocational education. Again, the award depends in almost all cases on assessments made within the school: it is based on systematic half-yearly reports, and discussions in the group of teachers of the class, in years 5-9 or 10; and these reports are based on a prescribed number of internal school tests. Pupils must be given due notice of the time and subject matter of such tests as well as information about marks awarded for other aspects of their work. Teachers must keep systematic records and inform both pupils and the headteacher of the spread of marks in their tests and other assessments. As at other levels, teachers' marks may be queried or challenged by pupils or parents.

A departure from internal school assessment is found in Bavaria which awards two types of final certificate to those completing year 9 of the *Hauptschule*. One is based on the normal internal assessment by the school and certifies satisfactory completion of the course. The other, the "qualifying" *Hauptschule* certificate, is awarded on the results of an exam set externally by the local authority. Its possession qualifies for entry to year 10 of the *Realschule* or to higher forms of vocational training as well as being useful in applying for employment. Similarly, in Bavaria the *Realschule* leaving certificate is awarded on the basis of a central examination.

Abitur

The *Abitur* certificate, the qualification for entry to higher education, was first established some two hundred years ago (though made available to girls considerably later). Completion of studies in a *Gymnasium* which it signified was intended to develop a liberal, many-sided European culture. Many variations have taken place in both the *Gymnasium* and the *Abitur* during the last two centuries and in recent years some doubts have emerged as to the value of academic studies. Until recently, over 90 per cent of those gaining the *Abitur* intended to proceed to university: nowadays some 70 per cent may have this intention. North-Rhine-Westphalia is experimenting with upper secondary schools which combine vocational subjects with general subjects so that students can gain either a vocational *Abitur* (giving entry to institutions of higher vocational education) or the general, traditional *Abitur*. Some Länder award alternative certificates, valid only within the Land, notably to pupils who have not studied a second foreign language. But the general *Abitur* remains the much sought-after hallmark of German education.

The most dramatic changes in *Abitur* curriculum and assessment have taken place within the last twenty years. Following an agreement of the KMK in 1972, a new structure was introduced in 1976/77 for school work in years 11-13, the upper secondary stage (with students normally at ages 16-19). Instead of the earlier lockstep by which all members of a class studied the same subjects, individualised learning programmes were made possible by allowing students to choose subjects more widely and to decide, according to their own strengths and weaknesses, the level at which to study different subjects. The opportunity was also given to teachers to introduce new topics within their discipline (subject to the agreement of colleagues in their department). The award of the certificate was no longer to depend on final examinations but on a combination of examination and class-work assessments during years 12 and 13, year 11 serving as a preparatory year.

According to KMK agreement in 1988, students must in year 13 take examinations in two subjects at advanced level *(Leistungskurse)* and two at basic level *(Grundkurse)*. In three of these subjects they must take written exams: in one they have an oral exam only. (If their exam mark deviates greatly from their coursework record, they may also have an oral in that subject, or the student may ask for an oral in the hope of raising an exam mark.) But the candidate's total *Abitur* score is calculated by combining results gained in various courses during year 12 and year 13 with the results of the final exams. These coursework marks depend on a series of formal written tests as well as on the teacher's assessment of *"sonstige Mitarbeit"*, other work done for the class. In a remarkably complex way, the traditional 6-point scale is at this stage converted to a 15-point scale (by adding + and - marks to each of five levels, a mark of 6 counting as zero): and marks in different types of course are weighted (for example, points gained in advanced courses in year 12 are multiplied by 2). The number of points awarded for the actual final examinations is less than half the maximum possible points total of between 800 and 900. After the *Abitur* exam, the points total is converted, by an agreed conversion scale, to the familiar and better understood 6-point scale, though now with decimal points added: the "ideal mark" of 1.0 is sometimes achieved.

Students' freedom to choose the subjects of their individual programmes is admittedly limited by KMK regulations -- a circumstance which led to some student dissatisfaction in the early years when the promised new freedom proved to be less than expected. Subjects are divided into three main areas: languages-literature-arts (including German, art, music and a number of foreign languages); social sciences (history, geography, social studies, law, philosophy, psychology, education); mathematics-science-technology (the sciences offered include domestic science and data-processing). Religion (or appropriate alternative) and sport are categorised separately and are compulsory for varying amounts of time but can also be taken as advanced courses, within specific conditions. Students in the preparatory year 11 have a large number of compulsory subjects and some optional: choices of advanced courses begin in the second half of this year. Students must then continue to include at least one course from each of the three main areas in their choice of subjects and observe various regulations about taking, in addition to their chosen advanced courses, the required number of basic (possibly half-yearly) courses in appropriate combinations. If the *Gymnasium* does not offer teaching in a subject the student wants -- such schools still specialise in emphasis, for example, in humanistic subjects or in science -- it may be possible to take it in a neighbouring *Gymnasium*. (Time-tabling for both staff and students has become more complicated as a result of these curricular reforms.) A counselling service is provided in the schools to help students plan their programmes and ensure that their choices accord with regulations.

The role of the individual teacher continues to be dominant in *Abitur* assessments. Two Länder set *Abitur* exam questions centrally, using themes proposed by their teachers. But in the other Länder it is the teacher who prepares two or three sets of questions for the class which has been taught. These questions are submitted to the state's education authority early in the year. The teacher has to explain how they relate to what has been taught and what responses are expected. In some cases, questions may be referred back to the scrutineers (usually retired heads or subject experts from teacher education) for further discussion and modification but it is rare for questions to be rejected. The authority then selects one of the sets prepared and informs the school, shortly before the exam, which set is to be used. In teaching and in setting questions, the teacher has to keep in mind KMK guidance about the qualities to be developed in pupils: receptiveness, acquisition of knowledge; ability to use knowledge in new conditions; judgement of what has been studied. In the different subject areas, illustrative examples and discussions of possible test questions have been provided by the KMK or the Land. Guidance is also given to teachers as to the differences to be expected between advanced and basic exam standards.

Except in one Land which circulates *Abitur* exam papers to be marked by other schools, the *Abitur* papers are marked by the candidates' own teacher. For the written examinations, a system of dual marking is used, a colleague from the same department checking the marks given by the class teacher. The distribution of marks is, as in other examining, open to public scrutiny: and samples of scripts are called in for checking by some Land authorities.

For the oral examination, regulations determine the amount of time (not more than 30 minutes) candidates may have to prepare their answers to the question set and the amount of time to be given to the second part of the examination when they engage in discussion with the examiner(s). In a typical oral exam, the "jury" can consist of four people belonging to the candidates' school, one of whom, the class teacher, puts the questions, though this may also be done by the jury's chair (usually the school head); a third member records the proceedings; the fourth observes. Normally, three of the jury would be teachers of the subject being examined. The mark is to be agreed by all the examiners -- if there is continuing disagreement (reportedly very rare), the chair has a casting vote.

As at other levels of school assessment, candidates have the right of appeal to the central authority of the state.

The *Abitur* mark becomes particularly important when students want to enter one of the *numerus clausus* faculties in universities. The number of places in such subjects as medicine and sciences is, for various reasons, limited: the *Abitur* thus becomes a selective instrument, those with the best marks gaining the coveted places. (There was for some years considerable controversy about the traditional absolute entitlement of *Abitur* holders to enter university and this modern reduction of that right: an attempt was made to prove the refusal of places unconstitutional.) For some years also there was concern that candidates' marks were not comparable: marking was evidently more generous in some Länder than in others: consequently for a short period of time a system of *bonus* and *malus* points was used, increasing by a few decimal points the marks of candidates from "hard-marking" states, and decreasing the marks of those from the more generous. But now a quota system has been introduced for *numerus clausus* subjects, depending on the number of applicants from each Land: within that quota, candidates compete with those of their own Land on the basis of *Abitur* marks (to gain a place in medicine, for example, may require 1.2): but some credit is also given for "waiting time".

Issues

The German system of education offers an interesting example of decentralisation at national level (though with common agreement on some issues) combined with curricular centralisation at the level of individual states (which vary considerably in size) and with decentralisation to school level of much of the assessment of pupils. Greater national centralisation may be accepted in the near future as a by-product of concern for equalisation of provision in the "new" East German states and as a result of the general process of harmonization of qualifications in the European Community, particularly in the sphere of vocational education. At the same time, the respect for *Kulturhoheit* remains firmly entrenched. Especially in the structure and administration of school systems, Land autonomy, with strong political influences, seems likely to continue. Within each Land there are, despite some recent eliminations of long-outdated requirements, astonishingly large numbers of ministerial regulations determining the work of the schools. Perhaps because so many aspects are centrally controlled by the Land, there seems little inclination to reduce the amount of decentralisation evident in individual schools' and teachers' freedom to make assessments of their pupils' work.

Important issues in assessment fall into two categories: (a) possible effects of the assimilation of the "new" East German states, (b) characteristics of the existing West German systems.

Assimilation of the former East German states

The patterns of school structure introduced by the former East German states could encourage changes in structure and consequent changes in the functions of assessment throughout the country. Controversy about differentiated secondary education has characterised West German education, both with regard to the age level at which differentiation should begin and with regard to the provision of secondary education in differentiated or integrated schools. Decisions on these points, according to the policy of the individual Länder, determine the points at which assessment has important effects on pupils' whole experience of education. The assimilation of the East German states adds to this debate since they have to transform a system which consisted of a 10-year comprehensive school, beginning at age 6, followed either by a selective two-year academic school leading to the *Abitur* (highly selective not only on academic merit but in accordance with manpower planning and the political background of pupils) or by vocational education, or by a three-year course combining vocational qualification with an *Abitur*. Thus, some 10-year schools may extend upwards to *Abitur* level while remaining comprehensive schools: the two-year upper secondary school may become a *Gymnasium*, providing not only for classes 11 and 12, but also for classes 9 and 10 -- ultimately, perhaps, becoming a six-year *Gymnasium* for classes 7 to 12.

If the former East German states were to maintain the common school at least until the end of class 6, pupils in that part of Germany would continue to be spared selective assessment at the age of 10 and possibly the example of the former East German states might encourage a similar postponement of selective assessment in some of the former West German systems where such selection now occurs. Thus, some progress would be made towards reducing a rather unsatisfactory instance of assessment -- unsatisfactory when dealing with 10-year-olds, no matter how it is carried out. But unfortunately, in this respect, it appears that the majority of the "new states" are going to adopt patterns similar to those of the majority of the former West German states: so what could have been a beneficial effect of the assimilation of East German education is unlikely to occur.

The importance of assessment at other levels also seems likely to continue, the more so as the former East German states are under pressure to introduce more differentiation in the curriculum before class 10. Nevertheless, the significance of assessment will depend to a considerable extent on whether curricular differentiation is to occur within schools or in schools of different types. The maintenance and growth of comprehensive schools in the East German Länder might encourage the development of more comprehensive schools in the country as a whole, with a consequent reduction in the importance of selective assessment: yet this seems doubtful, since there are strong feelings against such schools in some West German Länder. Thus, assessment for entry to differentiated schools will probably continue to need attention, as will procedures for transfer to another school when assessment seems to have been inaccurate.

Emphasis on maintaining the high standards of the *Abitur* -- and the East German states have committed themselves to assimilation *(Anschaltung)* at this level by 1994 -- must reinforce selective assessment between or within schools. The present structure of the *Abitur* shows an interesting combination of the attempt to combine respect for students' freedom of choice with protection of the curricular ideal of a broad and balanced programme of study. But it remains uncertain whether the present balance will be maintained or whether the wish to ensure high standards for entry to universities will lead to increased restriction on choice, with more subjects, or certain subject combinations, becoming compulsory -- thus increasing, by KMK agreement, central determination of the curriculum.

There is an associated question of whether the East German states should make the full academic course of education last for 13 years rather than 12. Some West German educators would rather prefer to reduce their traditionally long period of schooling to the 12 years customary in other countries. But while this might entail curricular changes, the assessment system seems unlikely to be affected.

The future impact of assessment will also depend on how much weight is really given to the affirmations made in the "new" Länder that the wishes of parents and students will be respected: and on the extent to which this principle becomes more widespread in the "old" Länder. Some incompatibility between reduction of assessment in order to give more open access in secondary education and reliance on assessment to support national and Land aspirations for high vocational and academic standards could produce further problems.

Again there is the question of changes to be made in East German teacher education and the impact on this education of curriculum changes in the schools which have produced increased demands for teachers of English, an excess supply of teachers of Russian, and a revival of the teaching of Latin. Meanwhile, there are the problems of enabling teachers accustomed to the East German assessment system, with marking on the Soviet model, and with pressures encouraging upward drift, to adapt to the traditional West German assessment procedures.

West Germany

The position of West German teachers with regard to assessment shows remarkable freedom since they set tests and exams for their own pupils, mark them and take responsibility for recommendations about the pupils' future progress -- admittedly, while remaining accountable to colleagues, parents and pupils. Teachers assess what they have taught their classes while following the curriculum centrally defined by the Land. (It is however interesting that changes in the upper secondary curriculum were introduced and supported by changes -- agreed at federal level -- in assessment for the *Abitur*; and that for the *Abitur* there is also some federal guidance as to the principles on which the curriculum must be based.) The traditional West German system thus depends on the professional competence of teachers to make fair and reliable assessments: it gives teachers a professional recognition which might with advantage be introduced in other systems. The competence of individual schools to assess their pupils' work is also recognised in that, in almost all Länder, the certificate for completion of junior secondary education (at the end of class 9 or class 10) is awarded on the basis of internal school assessment.

Such confidence must of course be based on a thorough preparation for teaching. (It may be recalled here that a *Gymnasium* teacher's first appointment to a permanent post will not be until age 25, assuming smooth progress is made through the stages of teacher education: *Abitur* at 19, four years at university, to first state exam, two years as *Referendar*, with second state examination.) Yet it is not entirely clear whether this thorough preparation gives sufficiently detailed attention to the study of assessment procedures or whether teachers are rather left to pick up this skill by observation during the preparatory period and by experience. Assessment of *"sonstige Mitarbeit"*, evaluation of pupils' other contributions to the work of the class, seems in particular to be an area where uncertainties may remain as to what should be considered and receive credit.

There may also be undue pressures on teachers by parents who are anxious to ensure that their children gain satisfactory marks. And since the assessment procedure is so open, there may be a temptation for teachers to confine tests to material which can be objectively assessed so that the mark given can easily be explained and defended. Teachers too may lack awareness of the standards reached in other schools by comparable classes -- this is of course a matter of concern also from the point of view of ensuring equality of educational opportunity. Some guidance in such respects may come from provision made by the individual Land: but more information, either quantitative or qualitative, about standards achieved by pupils in other schools might be helpful to the German teachers.

Some other useful features of the West German assessment procedures may be noted. At primary level, some attempts are made to assess not only work in the subjects taught but also children's attitudes to learning and to social situations: development of this approach would seem advantageous, together with enhanced in-service training for teachers in this kind of assessment. It is also important that attention is given to the ability to express knowledge and opinions orally; and that at *Abitur* level the attempt is made to ensure fairness and impartiality in the process of oral examining. The danger, often mentioned in international discussion of assessment, that oral exams may be subjective and unfair, is guarded against here by detailed definitions of the conditions of the exam and by such devices as preparatory meetings of the examiners. (Recognition of the importance of oral examining is of course also found in various other European education systems, though uncommon in British schooling.)

Another useful aspect of West German assessment is that it is frequently based not on one examination or test but on the pupil's performance during the year or over a longer period, for example the two-year basis of assessment at *Abitur* level. Yet this continuous assessment apparently can also foster in some pupils and parents excessive attention to, and anxiety about, school marks. Much depends, obviously, on the importance of the outcome for the individual, whether allocation to differentiated schooling or entry to a preferred next stage of education is involved, or whether assessment is simply to lead to certification of satisfactory completion of a stage of education. In the West German system, it is perhaps regrettable that serious consequences, like allocation to differentiated schools, affect relatively young children and adolescents: as has been suggested, it is perhaps a restructuring of secondary education rather than major changes in assessment that would be most beneficial to the pupils.

A party of English Inspectors who studied curriculum and assessment in West Germany in the mid-1980s commented that the assessment system seemed remarkably inexpensive in comparison with the examination industry in England and Wales but that there were of course the hidden costs of extensive teacher education, (relatively) high teacher pay, and resources devoted to schools and curriculum development. Reliance on teacher judgement does require a well educated teaching body which enjoys high status. Given these factors (though recent teacher unemployment has had adverse effects on the status of the profession in Germany), it is easy to comprehend the lack of enthusiasm among some German educators for test norms and standardization, and their view that such products are an attempt to put into a rigid framework human beings who are individuals and capable of using their own independent judgement.

REFERENCES

DEPARTMENT OF EDUCATION AND SCIENCE (1987), *Education in the Federal Republic of Germany: Aspects of curriculum and assessment.* London: HMSO.

DER BUNDESMINISTER FÜR BILDUNG UND WISSENSCHAFT (1991), *Grund- und Struktur-Daten, 1990-91.* Bonn.

HÖRNER, W. (1990), *Bildung und Wissenschaft in der DDR: Ausgangslage und Reform bis Mitte 1990.* Bonn: Bundesminister für Bildung und Wissenschaft.

KRAUS, J. (ed.)(1990), *Schule und Lehrerberuf: Eine Materialien- und Aufsatzsammlung für Lehrer und Bildungspolitiker in den neuen deutschen Ländern,* 3 Auflage, November. Bonn: Deutscher Lehrerverband.

SCHULTZ, D. (1988), "The school system in the Federal Republic of Germany". Ruhr-Universität Bochum, mimeo.

Chapter 4

THE NETHERLANDS

by
Professor Margaret Sutherland
University of Leeds

Educational research and development in the Netherlands has the advantage of support by three government-funded institutions, the Foundation for Educational Research (SVO), the National Institute for Curriculum Development (SLO) and the National Institute for Educational Measurement (CITO). CITO, established by the Dutch Ministry of Education and Science in 1968, provides the education system with a remarkable range of expertly constructed tests - tests for diagnostic purposes, for selection, for certification, for monitoring individual learners' progress and for monitoring national standards in education.

The national system

The Dutch education system provides eight years of primary education for children aged between 4 and 12, an Education Act of 1985 having merged the former upper kindergarten classes with primary schools. Education is compulsory from age 5 to age 16 (tuition is free up to age 16) but in practice most children begin primary school at age 4. Secondary education is provided in four types of school: Junior Secondary Vocational Schools (LBO), Junior General Secondary Schools (MAVO), Senior General Secondary Schools (HAVO), Pre-university Secondary Schools (VWO). LBO and MAVO give four years of education, HAVO, five, and VWO six years. There is thus a problem of selection (or guidance) into differentiated secondary education at age 12, even though in principle the first year of secondary education is regarded as a transition stage and some later transfers to different types of school are possible (see Figure 3).

Since 1920, the Dutch education system has constitutionally given considerable freedom to groups of parents or others to establish schools in accordance with their own religious or philosophical views. Such schools, provided they comply with certain conditions and regulations (for example regulations concerning teacher qualifications and conditions of work), receive the same funding from the government as do schools provided by the local education authorities. In fact, some 70 per cent of pupils attend "private" schools. This cherished freedom of education means that there is, at primary level, no centralised curriculum; but all primary schools must provide tuition in the subjects included in an official list, that is, the content of their curricula is determined, but time allocation, choice of topics and methods, and

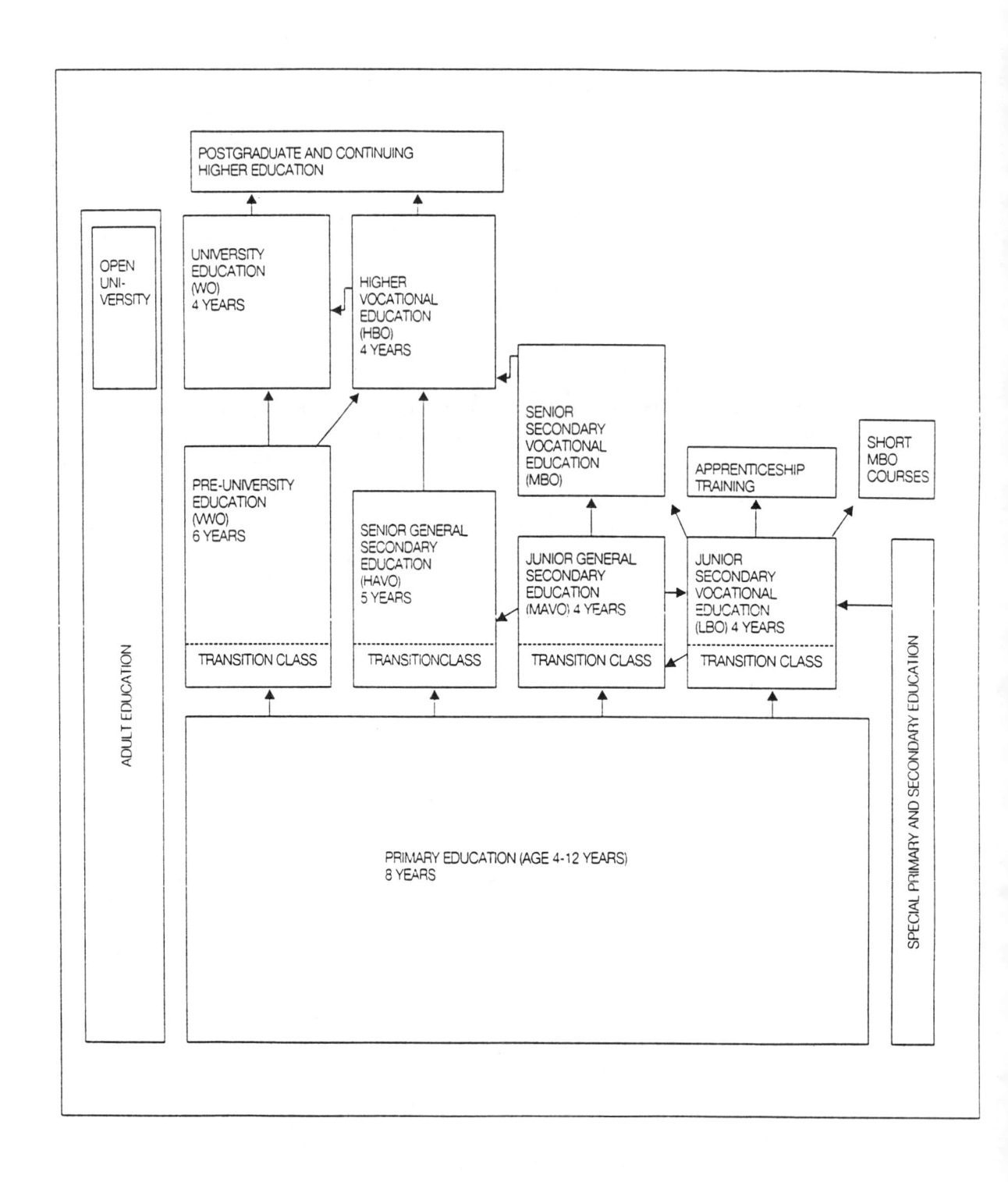

Figure 3: The education system in the Netherlands, 1991 (from the Kingdom of the Netherlands: Facts and Figures: Education and Science)

integration of subjects can be determined at local level. The authority responsible for the school or schools must produce at least every second year the official school work plan, according to guidelines given by the Primary Education Act, showing organisation, subject content, record-keeping and methods of assessment. At secondary level, similarly there is an official statement of subjects to be taught and the numbers of hours to be spent on them; but as all schools participate in national examinations, the syllabus for such examinations has a considerable effect on much of what is taught.

National assessment

Proposals for assessing performance in the country's schools began to be heard in the 1970s but although some investigation of testing practices in the United States was carried out in 1979, opposition and expected opposition from various sources - political parties and teachers' unions, for instance - meant that the decision to embark on national assessment was delayed until 1986 when the Dutch National Assessment Programme in Primary Education (PPON) was brought into existence to be implemented by CITO. The idea of blanket testing has not been entertained. Assessment is carried out on carefully drawn samples of about 200 schools each year. In sampling, attention is given to three categories of school, categories determined by the weighting given by the authorities to decide how many teachers a school is entitled to have: for example, children of lower socio-economic groups are weighted at 1.25, ethnic minority children, 1.90. Almost half the schools in the sample are from the category with a weighting of 1.05 or less; about one-third from those between 1.06 and 1.15; and nearly 20 per cent from those with a weighting of over 1.15. Checks are made to ensure that the sample is balanced geographically and with respect to other relevant variables, but the main variable is the composition of the school population. Schools are not obliged to participate in this assessment procedure but as yet there have been few refusals from schools proposed for inclusion in the chosen sample.

To allow time for the development of test items, testing has been carried out in different subjects in succeeding years: in 1987, in mathematics (mid-primary and end-of-primary); in 1988, language (end-of-primary); in 1989, language (mid-primary); in 1990, social studies and physical geography; in 1991, science/health education, English, traffic education. In each subject area, a domain specification is made. Care is taken not to concentrate only on a "core curriculum" within the subject but to include aspects which may be taught by only some of the schools. In this way, it is hoped to encourage wider development of the subjects in question.

In addition to the items designed to discover pupils' attainment in a given subject, information is gathered from the schools concerning the amount of time given to the subject and the topics included when it is taught; there are also questionnaires as to the characteristics and attitudes of the schools and the pupils. Such information, made available to schools, helps them to "stock-take" their own timetabling and teaching practices: it can indicate relationships between performance and the teaching experienced.

It is emphasized by those engaged in this assessment that their function is not to be judgemental but simply to provide a mirror of what is happening in the schools. At the same time, the absence of criteria of attainment can make it difficult to interpret the results. Therefore, information has been obtained from groups of parents and groups of primary and secondary teachers as to what they would have expected or hoped for in pupils' attainment in the areas assessed. This information has also been included in reports so that it can contribute to ongoing debates about the curriculum. (Reports, it may be noted, are of three kinds: technical reports; reports produced for the information of professionals - that is, for people in the education-support agencies, for inspectors, for those engaged in teacher-training; and booklets summarising the main findings, which are sent to all schools and their governing bodies.)

Some further characteristics of the assessment procedure deserve attention. Trained assistants are used in the administration of the tests. Only one half-day per school is used for testing and each pupil will give only one hour to the procedure - not all items are taken by each school and each pupil. The items have been pre-tested and analysed. Care is taken to avoid, where possible, multiple-choice questions since it is recognised that many educators are hostile to this format: in the first mathematics tests over 90 per cent of items were open-ended.

Those who construct the tests are aware of their possible influence on schools' teaching policies though such an influence would seem beneficial if schools' awareness of what can be taught is increased and if good approaches currently found in only a minority of schools are spread more widely in this way. But an assessment of the performance of individual schools cannot be made as children within them will be taking different test items; and the children themselves are anonymous. The outcomes of national assessment simply show the overall levels of performance in different domains of the subject tested. To provide some schools with information they might like to have, some experimental work with a "local service option" has been done: schools which participated in the national assessment were allowed to use in the year following the national assessment a selection of the maths items with their current year's grade 8 classes; they were then able to compare their pupils' performance with the national norms. This kind of development could be expanded.

As for national assessment surveys in secondary education, CITO has been commissioned to execute a few surveys on an experimental basis, at the junior secondary level. Decisions about a possible introduction of such assessment on a regular basis will be taken after the results of the work being done at present are reported.

Assessment at primary school level: monitoring pupils' progress

Diagnostic testing, especially in the lower forms of primary schools, has been quite common for a long time. Such tests have been developed by universities and local agencies: they have also been produced commercially. When CITO was established in 1986, it also began to develop different kinds of tests for the primary school level. Since then, it has been producing tests for many purposes, including monitoring, in addition to its work for the assessment of the quality of education nation-wide. For example, some studies of children's abilities from age 4 onwards in arithmetic, spatial orientation and movement in space have been carried out, mainly to facilitate early discovery of children with learning difficulties. Since diagnosis by these tests seemed to indicate the need for further action, a programme of remedial teaching was devised, following on the test findings.

In association with intensified government policies for earlier identification of under-achieving children, and with the aim of reducing referrals to special education, CITO has been developing a comprehensive set of tests for the whole primary school age range. The initial development has been in the Rotterdam area where there is a large migrant population. Individual pupils' progress could now be effectively studied and facilitated by the general use of these tests.

So far, the tests have been constructed in language, arithmetic and information-processing: others are being developed in other subject areas. These tests can be given two or three times a year. Ingeniously, test modules have been developed so that after the first module is worked through, the teacher can give the next higher module to the stronger pupils and the next lower to the weaker. Pupils' scores are interpreted by a standardized scale. It is thus possible to compare the individual's performance against the norms for that class level. Consecutive testing shows whether the pupil is maintaining steady progress, improving or falling into the danger area of deteriorating performance which calls for remedial intervention. Computer software has been developed to inform the teacher about the tests, analyse pupils' scores and show subject domains in which weakness is present as well as the trend of the individual pupils' performances. It is also planned to make it possible for pupils to do tests interactively with the computer rather than use test booklets. (It is estimated that by 1994 all schools will have the appropriate computers, but some time may elapse before the computers are in effective use.)

In association with these tests, "help-books" are being produced for teachers who want to give remedial or revision lessons to some pupils or to the class group. The contents of these booklets have been developed in association with groups of teachers and the explanatory material indicates different ways in which these aids can be used, including the development of learning skills in the pupils.

At present it is for individual schools and teachers to decide whether to use the tests or the accompanying teaching materials, though during the experimental development the Rotterdam authority's schools had to use them. Some anxiety has been expressed by teachers who fear that if results of such testing become publicly known or are collected by a central school authority, they may be misinterpreted, especially when schools have a large proportion of disadvantaged children.

A shorter-term monitoring of pupils' progress is facilitated by a test available for children in year 7, that is, in the penultimate year of primary education (though it can also be used for pupils in the first year of junior vocational schools). The test scores again give information about the pupil's performance in aspects of language use, arithmetic and information-processing. The teacher can obtain from the test information as to weaknesses and strengths of individual pupils and also an indication of the whole class's performance in relation to national or regional norms. CITO's intention here would be to encourage remedial teaching where it seems necessary but there is some doubt as to whether this consequence usually follows. This test, since it is diagnostic only, is not renewed yearly but at intervals of five or six years.

Assessment for selection

At age 12, at the end of year 8 of the primary school, pupils proceed to the four different types of secondary education. To assist in selection procedures, CITO provides a 180-item test of language, arithmetic and information-processing. It is administered on two school days. A new test is provided every year for this purpose from item banks which are continuously being replenished - for example, to include new items corresponding to new teaching in arithmetic. These items are produced by a combination of CITO researchers and trained teachers who receive some payment for their work. Since very large numbers of scripts have to be marked in a short period of time, multiple-choice answers are used here.

The pupils' total scores on the test have been found to be better predictors than individual subject scores: but in addition to the pupil's standardized total score, the report on each pupil taking the test shows the number of correct answers in each of the three subjects and the pupil's percentile rank in each. An accompanying diagram shows for each of the four types of school the percentage of pupils there having had the same or a lower standardized score, or a higher score than this pupil. In this way it is indicated to all concerned what the pupil's chances of success are likely to be in the different school types - for example, if a pupil had scored 536, in MAVO 33 per cent of pupils would have had a higher score; in VWO, 93 per cent would have a higher score; but only 11 per cent in LBO.

Teachers also have to give an estimate of pupils' suitability for different types of schooling at this point and research indicates that teachers' estimates may be slightly higher in predictive value than test results (0.81 compared with 0.76), though not for all sub-groups. While the primary school gives advice and parents may have wishes as to the type of school they want for their children, it is ultimately the secondary school which decides whether to accept a pupil or not. But the situation is complicated by the fact that combinations of different school types are available - LBO/MAVO, for example, or MAVO/HAVO, or MAVO/HAVO/VWO or HAVO/VWO. Such "mixed" types may be flexible about their acceptance of pupils and a great deal also depends on the locality in which the pupil is living. Combinations of schools are in fact likely to become more frequent in future but meanwhile some combinations and some types of school are more rigorously selective than others. The only school types for which an approved level of entrance qualification is legally essential are HAVO and VWO.

The situation is further complicated by the fact that primary schools can choose whether to use the CITO test *(Eindtoets Basisonderwijs)* or not. In practice, some 60 per cent of schools do use it. Those schools which do not use the CITO test may instead use an intelligence test, though such a test costs more than the CITO test: preferences for the two types of test tend to vary according to regions of the country. Alternatively, an achievement test developed by a local educational support agency may be used. A small minority of schools, about 10 per cent, do not give any test: in such cases the children are likely to be going to LBO and parents are not keenly interested in the allocation.

On the other hand, some schools do use test booklets of preceding years as material for coaching their pupils in preparation for the selection test. Despite research findings that coaching for more than five or six hours does not improve scores, some teachers persist in this kind of preparation. There is, however, a preparatory booklet which can be bought by the school and used to familiarise pupils with the test structure.

It must be recalled that in principle the first year of secondary school is a transition period. MAVO, HAVO and VWO schools have to teach the same subjects for a prescribed number of hours per week, though a modified timetable is prescribed for LBO schools. But the content and rate of progress of such teaching will vary: there is also the possibility that in mixed type schools, streaming will begin even in this first year. Thus, the selective effect of the test taken at the end of primary school is very strong.

In general, entry to a specific type of secondary school remains important because, although attempts are now being made to reduce differences between schools in the early years of secondary education and to set common attainment targets for a core curriculum, substantial differences are likely to remain, particularly with regard to the age at which the targets are reached. While later transfers to other school types are possible, pupils moving "upwards" are likely to need an extra year to reach the level of their new school.

Assessment for certification

External secondary school examinations, leading to appropriate leaving certificates, are taken at ages 16, 17 and 18. The Ministry of Education and Science entrusts a standing committee (CEVO) with the responsibility of deciding on the contents and standards; but the construction of the examinations and processing their results are delegated to CITO, which has an Examinations Department for these purposes. CITO also has a Department for Senior Secondary Education which constructs some tests (mainly in languages and science) for use on a voluntary basis in secondary schools and develops item banks and other forms of assistance to schools wishing to do their own testing. Both CITO Departments also engage in research.

Certificate examinations are of importance to pupils since they serve to give qualification for entry to senior secondary vocational education rather than apprenticeship training, for transfer to general senior secondary schools, and for entry to university: at the same time they certify the successful completion of a stage of education. As in other countries, the two functions, certifying completion and attempting prediction, may conflict, since they can be better served by different types of examinations.

A notable development since 1983 has been the introduction of differentiated papers in the external examinations at 16+, the lower level designated as C, the higher as D. For transition to higher forms of secondary education, a prescribed number of subjects has to be taken at D level.

Considerable technical expertise has had to be used by CITO to produce valid differentiation here since no specific criteria had been offered.

Considerable expertise also goes to ensuring the comparability of the external examinations from year to year and to determining the correct cut-off point for passing and failing - CEVO is formally responsible for the latter. Much attention has been given to finding the best type of question: although objective, multiple-choice questions have clear advantages for the speedy marking required, open-ended questions are also used, the latter being marked, with guidance, by teachers in schools. For LBO and MAVO, objective questions and mixed format questions are included: in HAVO and MAVO examinations open-ended questions alone are preferred in some subjects. At all levels, languages (apart from Latin and Greek) are tested by objective questions. Where an exam has consisted of objective questions, the school receives not only individual candidates' marks but a survey showing the school means in comparison with national means.

Perhaps the most controversial matter is the Dutch system of using both internal and external assessment for the award of certificates. The exams set and processed by CITO give a mark (on a scale of 1 to 10) for each candidate in the subjects taken. Each school also produces a subject mark for each candidate. An arithmetical mean is calculated to provide the candidate's final mark in each subject. The school's mark depends entirely on procedures within the individual school, so there may well be differences between schools in the content and methods of assessment. Studies in recent years have indicated that the percentage of fail marks in HAVO and VWO was greater in the external exam results than in the final average mark list.

The problems arising from such combination of marks arrived at by different methods are obvious. Teachers complain that their judgement, based on long-term knowledge of the candidates' work, is distorted by a mark based on a one-off external exam (sometimes using objective questions only). But they also complain that the average mark gives less useful information to higher education institutions than would differentiated marks. There is certainly the problem that assessment is being used for more than one purpose. Yet precisely because there are so many arguments on both sides, the combination of internal and external assessment seems likely to remain.

Important future tasks for CITO will result from implementation of proposals to introduce common attainment targets for junior secondary education. Some work has already been done on possible test constructions, allowing for a variety of modes of assessment and for collaboration between individual schools and the central testing agency. But again the absence of clearly defined criteria may create problems.

Other assistance to teachers

CITO-produced tests can help teachers to monitor the effects of their teaching on learners' progress and to know how their class compares with classes elsewhere. Further innovations have been started on a more or less experimental basis, involving the use of microcomputers and other modern media. CITO is creating item banks for different subjects taught in secondary schools. Using microcomputers, schools can draw on these resources to create their own school tests. The package offers information on difficulty level of items, domains covered and analysis of students' performance. But since the freedom to choose their own curricula is so cherished by schools, it is possible for the school to add to the items which CITO has produced (on the basis of general agreement as to relevance) the school's own test items - though the school cannot modify or delete the CITO items.

Other work done by CITO's Department of Vocational Education can also be of assistance to teachers in general education, for example its publication of a brochure on the structure and assessment of tests of practical skills and its study of the assessment of skills in interviewing.

Issues

Provision made here shows how different forms of assessment can be used for different purposes - monitoring, selection, certification, as well as evaluation of national standards in education. Materials have been constructed to help teachers to compare their pupils' progress with that of others, to be aware of the various domains to be attended to within subjects and to use a selection of scientifically constructed test items as part - but only a part - of their teaching programme. The scope, sophistication and general expertise of these provisions offer most useful models for development in other countries. It is also remarkable that whereas hostility to national assessment was present when the proposals for it were first made, this hostility seems largely to have died away as experience showed the procedures not to have the effects feared. Some questionnaire evidence indicates a favourable response to national testing so far as schools are concerned. (It is to be remembered that the national testing does not report on, or single out, the performance of individual schools or teachers.)

In some ways it could be argued that assessment in the Netherlands is too good for the system in which it operates - or, more accurately, that assessment could operate more effectively still if some reforms in the present education system were to take place.

The system has long been beset with proposals to introduce a comprehensive system of junior secondary education and with determined opposition to the introduction of such a system. The removal of selective transition to secondary education would produce new attitudes to assessment in the primary school. While the efficiency of structure of end-of-primary tests is admirable, there is, as in other countries, some misguided coaching for them: and there is the curious variable introduced by some schools' decisions not to use these tests. If selection at this age level were eliminated, both schools and CITO could usefully concentrate more on diagnostic and monitoring activities. Similarly, the reform of junior secondary education might reduce some of the importance attached to final examinations there. A major complication is the admirable principle of the freedom of individual schools, a freedom re-emphasized in the 1987 Law on support services. Schools therefore decide to what extent they wish to buy and use tests of various kinds. They are also not obliged to participate in the National Assessment Programme - even if, in practice, they usually do. Again, in secondary school assessment, while schools do have to present pupils for the external examinations, they produce also their own assessments, and so arises the controversy about the validity of school mark and test mark. The freedom actually enjoyed by individual schools may be exaggerated - in practice, many similarities and conformities emerge - but the remarkably large number of school authorities in a relatively small country is astonishing. While the principle of schools' freedom remains as a political rallying-point in debates on education, it can, paradoxically enough, impede apparently desirable developments in teaching and assessment.

Nevertheless, at various points it is clear that centrally-produced assessment can affect the curriculum, both in the elementary school and in the secondary school. The National Assessment Programme's testing is likely to be influential: teachers receiving information about other schools' practices in teaching and noting the contents of test items are very likely to adapt their own teaching accordingly. End-of-primary and/or monitoring tests similarly may introduce ideas for change in teaching. At secondary level external examination items will guide teaching in schools; and the tests produced by the Secondary Education Department for various subjects will influence work in schools voluntarily using them. But the major effects on curriculum seem to come rather from the gradual restructuring of secondary education by the listing and time-tabling of core subjects. Given existing respect for school freedom, direct curriculum development tends to be concentrated on projects in pilot schools and other experimental work. SLO also co-ordinates curriculum development in other areas and establishments; but while it maintains a national register of teaching aids and provides guidelines concerning them, it does not produce complete curricular materials for national use.

There may of course be advantages in the operation of market forces where assessment tests are concerned. Test constructors ensure that tests look reasonable to teachers, that they are constructed in consultation with teachers, that they serve important purposes. But possibly the many education authorities are insufficiently aware of the contribution well-constructed tests can make to effective teaching and of the value of information showing a school's relative achievement - if such information is properly used (teachers' anxieties must be taken into account here). It may, however, also be the case that teacher education could develop clearer awareness of the value of various forms of assessment so that teachers perceive the advantages of expert advice and expertly constructed tests.

The provision at national level of three distinct organisations for education support (in addition to local educational and psychological services and regional pedagogical centres) is a distinctive feature of the Dutch system. The advisability of such separation could be questioned. In the past certainly there was some uncertainty as to the boundaries between the functions of research, assessment and curriculum development. But the 1987 Law, while introducing sharper definitions of their work, decided to maintain the continuing autonomy of the three organisations. It did however require co-ordination by means of meetings of the people responsible for them and co-ordination of the yearly programmes of work. Since there is awareness within the three organisations of what the others are doing, it does in fact seem that separate organisation is facilitating the best developments, concentrating resources and expertise and maintaining continuity of interest. This may be a rather typical and valuable instance of the principle of freedom of individual educational establishments.

The country of the Netherlands is fortunate in having an important scholarly community in the fields of psychometrics, sociometrics and social science methodology: such people, working in both universities and in CITO and other agencies, have an expertise which is internationally recognised. But the costs of developing testing in accordance with new technologies and research are very great. CITO is a non profit-making institution - and obviously the market for tests in a school system of the size it caters for can give only limited financial returns. At present, the proportions of funding to be used for assistance to schools, support work for ministerial innovations and for the organisation's own projects are approximately 2:2:1, but much depends on the total amount of government funding made available. This is indeed a problem common to many countries that, unless government policies are to provide adequate resources for the development of assessment procedures (and other aspects of education), the abilities and expertise of highly-qualified people will not be properly utilised and education systems will not produce the hoped-for results.

REFERENCES

CITO (nd), "Overview of the activities of the Department for Senior Secondary Education", Arnhem: CITO.

CITO (nd), "Overview of the activities of the Department of Examinations in Secondary Education", Arnhem: CITO.

CITO (nd), "Overview of the activities of the Department of Vocational Education", Arnhem: CITO.

KREEFT, H. P. J. and MOELANDS, H. A. (1991), *Examinering in het Voortgezet Onderwijs in vijf Europese landen: Een studie naar vergelijkingsmogelijkheden van examenresultaten van Nederland, Engeland, Frankrijk, West-Duitsland en Zweden*, Arnhem: CITO.

LUIJTEN, A. J. M. (ed) (1991), *Issues in Public Examinations: A Selection of the Proceedings of the 1990 IAEA Conference*, Utrecht: Lemma.

MINISTERIE VAN ONDERWIJS EN WETENSCHAPPEN (1987), *Onderwijsverzorging in Hoofdlijnen: Populaire Samenvatting van de Wet op de Onderwijsverzorging*, Zoetermeer, the Netherlands.

MINISTRY OF FOREIGN AFFAIRS, THE NETHERLANDS (nd), *The Kingdom of the Netherlands: Facts and Figures: Education and Science*.

MOELANDS, F., VAN DEN BOSCH, L. and GILLIJNS, P. (nd), Systematic evaluation: The pupil monitoring system, Arnhem: CITO.

SCHREIBER, W. H. and INGENKAMP, K. (eds) (1990), *International Developments in Large-scale Assessment*. Proceedings of the Symposium on Large-scale Assessment in an International Perspective, 16-18 June 1988, Deidesheim, West Germany. London: NFER-Nelson.

VAN KUYK, J. J. (nd), "A remediation model for the spatial orientation programme for infants", Arnhem: CITO.

WIJNSTRA, J. M. (1991), "PPON: The Dutch National Assessment Programme in Education", in McNicoll, D. R. (ed), *Large-scale Evaluation*, Consortium of Institutions for Development and Research in Education in Europe (CIDREE), Volume 3, pp 15-20. Enschede: National Institute for Curriculum Development.

Chapter 5

SPAIN

by
Professor John Nisbet
University of Aberdeen

The education system in Spain is undergoing its most radical reform for over 100 years. The reforms parallel political and economic changes, from centralised government to regional autonomy and from a rural to an industrial economy. In education, the major changes are in the curriculum, with potentially radical changes in educational assessment. The old system was strongly examination-oriented, with examinations each year in primary and secondary schools which pupils had to pass to avoid being held back *(repetir curso)*. "I seem to have spent my whole life in exams", was how one student teacher described her perception of her schooling. One aim in the reformed system is that assessment should be "a natural part of a self-regulatory system" (White Paper, 1990, p. 241), formative, integral to the educational process, delegated to teachers and schools, reducing the competitive element and limiting the *"repetir curso"*. The issue of how (or whether) this can be done makes Spain a particularly interesting case study.

The context for change

The process of modernising the curriculum began in 1969 with a White Paper *(Libro Blanco, La Educacion en España)* which aimed to create a unified system with equal opportunity instead of the existing "selection sieve" (Muñoz Sedano, 1987). The resulting 1970 proposals *(Orientaciones Pedagogicas)* introduced a structure in which basic general education (EGB) extended to age 14, followed by either a four-year programme of academic secondary education *(Bachillerato Unificado Polivalente,* BUP) or by vocational education. Though the proposals recommended a curriculum which emphasized the acquisition of learning skills rather than the accumulation of knowledge, the majority of schools continued in the traditional mode (Muñoz Sedano, 1987), and the failure rate continued high, 35 per cent of pupils failing to achieve the certificate at the end of EGB *(graduado escolar)*. After further proposals for reform in 1984, the Ministry of Education in 1987 sought to build a consensus on the lines of its comprehensive Project for Reform of Education, published as a basis for discussion. This proposed an experimental approach to reform: Javier Solana Madariaga, Minister of Education, describing the existing system as a "paralysing brake" on needed change, declared that "the proposals must be progressively introduced over a sustained period... and be argued and accepted by the whole of our society" (White Paper, 1990, p. 5). However, in the opinion of at least one critic, the debate has been superficial rather than profound:

> "The Spanish public is not much prepared or accustomed to debate on these themes, though this does not mean that they do not show interest in them. But there is practically no precise information to assess concrete aspects of the education system as a whole (except for statistical data on budgets, teachers and school ratios), so that the debate remains reduced to a contrast of principles, ideologies, political intentions, intuitions and impressions."

The picture is complicated by the delegation of political power to the "autonomous communities" in six regions, covering about 55 per cent of the population. These communities have formally been given "full powers" in the field of education: agreement on a national curriculum framework has involved lengthy negotiation, with anxiety that the proposals represent an erosion of autonomy and a return to central bureaucratic control. Some complain that too much is being left to the teachers; others that the reforms are being imposed by the central authorities on a bureaucratic model of innovation; both lines of criticism are an expression of the need for wider public participation. However, there has been extensive consultation involving professional, political and religious groups and parents' associations; the proposals are in general terms and provide for regional differences, in the attempt to achieve consensus on a framework to cover the whole country.

Consequently, recent years have seen a series of publications and decrees, culminating in 1990 and 1991 with agreement on a common framework *(Diseño curricular base)* for each stage and area of the curriculum, specifying minimal coverage *(decreto de enseñanzas minimas)*. This framework is expressed in general terms of objectives, "blocks" of content, and criteria for assessment, outlining method and approach, with the actual decisions on teaching and assessment being delegated to teachers and schools. Chapter 17 of the 1990 White Paper for the Reform of the Education System outlines the principles on which assessment should be based. The decrees of June 1991 *(Real Decreto* 1006/91, 1007/91 and annexes, *Boletin Oficial del Estado*, numero 152) specifying the regulations governing the curriculum, include detailed sections on procedures for assessment.

Assessment as a means of regulation

The intention is that the assessment system should contribute positively in shaping teaching and learning in the schools: it should "actively regulate the system and educational processes and not only passively assess or select students" (White Paper, p. 243). The function of assessment is thus essentially regulatory: "Education is self-regulatory, and assessment is a natural part, in its own right, of its self-regulatory system" (p. 241).

Two levels of assessment are distinguished, though they are closely inter-related: regulation of the educational system and regulation of the educational processes, that is, the assessment of pupils' learning. The first is seen as the responsibility of the education authorities; the second is, "in the first instance", the responsibility of the teachers and of the children themselves. The assessment of pupils during the compulsory years of schooling is done by teachers: there are no external examinations or tests. The proposals go further, introducing the idea of self-assessment by the pupils: "Pupils must learn to assess their own learning. Teachers and schools must be the agents who support assessment of their own activities, and the education authorities must develop adequate systems to assess how they function" (p. 243).

The assessment of pupils in examinations set by teachers is traditional: the concept of assessing the function of the system, other than by inspectors, is novel. The emphasis on self-regulation is an important element in the more general process of delegation of authority and in the move away from a rigid examination structure which would "distort and denaturalise... the processes and aims of education (p. 242), resulting in 'education for assessment' instead of 'assessment for education'". At the same time, it is recognised that: "The processes of self-assessment should be complemented... by other external assessment processes" (such as inspection) (p. 244). The assessment system which is envisaged is therefore based largely on continuous assessment rather than end-of-session examinations; it should be comprehensive in its coverage of all learning, flexible in serving diagnostic and remedial functions, and formative in its influence on the schools and pupils.

Monitoring the national system

Evaluation of the educational reforms will be based on evidence and recommendations from three sources: (i) a programme of testing and experimental design by the *Centro Nacional de Investigacion y Documentacion Educativa* (CIDE); (ii) reports from the educational inspectors nationally on how teachers are implementing the reforms; (iii) a new Institute of Research and Educational Assessment, the precise form of which has not yet been decided.

CIDE, a government unit located on the Madrid University campus, has the role of checking whether the general objectives of reform are being realised nationally. As there is no national examination structure, school examinations are being used to regulate pupils' progress through the education system, consequently CIDE develops its own tests in a range of subjects, based on the objectives specified in the reform proposals. These tests are mainly multiple-choice tests, on the model of the American Educational Testing Service, systematically constructed with statistical checks on validity and reliability. A sampling procedure is adopted for applying the tests, within a sophisticated pre-test post-test experimental design.

Evaluation of the reform programme by CIDE began in 1984, with three groups: an experimental group comprising classes in schools involved in the initial trials; internal control groups, other classes in the same schools; and external control groups, from a broad sample of 20 000 children, matched to provide equivalent groups. Five tests at secondary level and four at primary level were used, with additional data on related aspects (attitudes, social background, etc.). The evaluation was longitudinal, using two cohorts and three applications of tests at yearly intervals. Results have been published from 1988 on (Alvaro Page, 1988), and show that the performance of pupils in the experimental groups is generally comparable with those in the *Bachillerato* course of secondary education, superior in comprehension and poorer in mathematical computation, with more favourable attitudes to participation. But there are wide variations in average attainment between and within regions, and among different classes in each school.

This programme of evaluation takes up much of the limited resources of CIDE: the tasks of exploring alternative approaches to assessment and providing support for developing school-based assessment are not within its remit but are assigned to the new Institute which it is proposed to establish.

The role of the national inspectors in evaluating the system is specified in Chapter 14 of the 1990 White Paper. This is to be a major role for them, and their observations and comments will make an important contribution to evaluation of the reform proposals and to monitoring of the education system generally. (The fact that they report privately to the central authorities is seen by some critics as an element which will strengthen bureaucratic control.) The inspectors' evaluation will be guided by the "criteria for evaluation" set out in the 1991 decrees in some detail (though still in general terms). For example, in Language and Literature at the primary stage, the criteria for evaluation begin:

"1. To participate constructively (listen, respect others' opinions, reach agreement, offer reasoned opinions) in communication related to school activity (group work, debates, class assemblies, etc.) respecting the norms which make exchange possible in these situations;

2. To understand the meaning of oral texts ..."

There are 18 such criteria for Language and Literature, 18 for Knowledge of the Environment (Natural and Social), 15 for Creative Arts, etc, in primary education, and 24 for the Natural Sciences, 29 for the Social Sciences, 13 for Mathematics, 14 for Music, etc., in secondary education. The prime function of these criteria for evaluation, however, is to provide a focus for the teachers' tests in schools.

National testing is not on the agenda: there is no strong public demand for it (except perhaps some professional concern about allegedly declining standards): any general feeling is more likely to be a hostility born out of their own past experience of traditional schooling. Few people question the principle of reliance on the teachers' own tests (though they may wish to challenge teachers' decisions on their own children, as they are allowed to do).

The new Institute of Research and Educational Assessment will have advisory functions of proposing assessment models for the different levels, phases, areas and disciplines of the education system, advising regional authorities, developing assessment procedures applicable to schools, and encouraging evaluation studies of the education system. As yet, decisions on the form and structure of the Institute have been deferred. The role outlined in the White Paper (p. 260) is explicitly "limited to proposing assessment studies and models, carrying out assessments which the authorities have requested", and advising authorities and schools. Being thus dependent on authorities both for funding and for its programme, its credibility as an independent agency may perhaps be in doubt. The mechanism for translating the Institute's findings into improving teaching and learning is unspecified. While there is a commitment to developing self-assessment, the initiative for this remains under Ministry control:

> "The Institute of Educational Research and Assessment will also have to develop procedures and instruments for self-assessment of schools, which may serve as models to complement the assessments made by inspection or by external agents. The Ministry of Education and Science will stimulate the creation and development of these instruments" (p. 260).

Assessing the pupils

The assessment procedures set out in the 1990 White Paper and in the June 1991 decrees are the responsibility of the teachers, wholly internal to the schools, until university entrance at age 18. Since the prime function of assessing pupils is seen as regulation of the learning process, the emphasis is on formative assessment, providing guidance to pupils and teachers and shaping the pupils' approach to learning. Continuous assessment by teachers (with review and discussion within schools) is the means to this end at all stages in primary and secondary education:

> "Assessment should be part of the actual process of teaching and learning and should in no way be confined to isolated situations" (primary education, p. 248);

> "Assessment cannot and should not be limited to the correction of tests carried out in certain situations" (secondary education, p. 250).

This style of assessment makes extra demands on both teachers and pupils. Teachers have to plan appropriate assignments and mark them (and sometimes check each other's marking), and the assessment of course work is usually more time-consuming and more individual than traditional examination answers. For pupils, the burden of homework is increased (though this may be seen as an advantage), and there is a risk of stress in being on trial too frequently if the assessment is for "high stakes". Traditional examinations can be "managed" more comfortably, at least by the teachers; and multiple-choice tests provide marks more economically. But if they distort the teaching and learning, their convenience is no compensation.

In the Spanish reform, continuous assessment is intended to reflect the changing balance in the curriculum, with emphasis on evaluating learning processes and skills as well as knowledge. For example, the objectives specified in the June 1991 decrees include several which express this general aim:

> "to identify and pose questions and problems arising from daily experience, using knowledge and resources to resolve them creatively" (primary education, Decree 1006/91)

> "to work out strategies for identifying and resolving problems in the diverse fields of knowledge and experience, using procedures of intuition and logical reasoning, contrasting these and reflecting on the consequent process" (secondary education, Decree 1007/91).

Precise methods of designing assessment to test the achievement of these objectives are not specified: the intention is that they will be part of the continuous assessment by teachers, and thus will influence the pupils' learning.

"Assessment activities are enormously varied in both form and content" (p. 244), and therefore a variety of methods and approaches should be used, including self-assessment by pupils. The secondary stage especially should encourage pupils to be "progressively capable of self-assessment" (p. 251). The affective element in pupils' response to assessment is stressed, both at primary level, where it affects self-esteem and confidence, and in adolescence, when "the perception that young people have of themselves becomes of major importance in defining their personality and behaviour" (p. 251).

These proposals and decrees express a coherent philosophy of assessment which is humane, supportive and formative, interpreting "regulation" of the system in terms of development rather than of control, strikingly in contrast with the system which they aim to replace. How fully can they be implemented? Some critics, while approving the intention, query the feasibility of their operation and express reservations about the exclusive reliance on teachers' assessments up to the end of secondary education.

In the early years, assessment is informal, qualitative, based on observation, avoiding "the use of labels, marks or streaming" (p. 247). Primary education from ages 6 to 12 is divided into three cycles each of two years: assessment is internal, continuous, qualitative and orientating. At the end of each cycle, teachers review progress to identify necessary remedial programmes. At the end of the primary stage, the option remains open to hold a pupil back to repeat a year. But repeating should be "an exceptional occurrence" (p. 249), and this decision may be made only once (Decree 16421, Article 9). Provision is also made for a more flexible approach to assessment for pupils with special educational needs, and the limit on repeating a year applies also to them.

In secondary education from ages 12 to 16, this style of assessment continues throughout two two-year cycles, with review panels in schools to co-ordinate the ratings of specialist teachers. At this stage, teachers make more extensive use of written tests, and many schools retain the end-of-session tests. Again, there is an option at the end of each cycle to require a pupil to repeat a year, but this decision may be made only once in the course of secondary education.

Thus, over the period of compulsory education, the management of assessment is exclusively in professional hands. The pressures of external constraints begin to be more evident after the age of 16. In vocational education,

> "there is a demand for proof from the pupils... that they are really competent and capable of doing a profession... The connection between the technical-professional education system and the working world needs the development of a system of professional certificates which link the professional skills acquired with the demands of the productive system" (p. 254).

A structure of "flexible modules" is envisaged, with entrance requirements covering both general education (language, reasoning and, where necessary, calculus) and specific knowledge and skills.

For those pupils seeking university entrance through the *Bachillerato*, the continuing need for the traditional university entrance examination *(Selectividad)* is acknowledged, for a variety of reasons: to guarantee an appropriate level of attainment, to correct for differences between schools in order to ensure equal opportunity, and to operate the *numerus clausus* which restricts admissions to certain faculties. (Results are combined with the teachers' internal continuous assessments.) The *Selectividad* is thus the only external examination in the system, but, as a "high stakes" assessment, it is likely to exercise a strong influence on the later years of secondary education. The form of this examination, decided by the university authorities with Ministry approval, is designed to assess "academic maturity" as well as knowledge in subject areas. Academic maturity is defined in the White Paper as:

> "ability to organise, integrate, analyse and combine information, to resolve problems applying new skills and acquired knowledge and to obtain knowledge from an efficient use of plans and thought patterns... in short, the use of strategies for creating and thinking more than knowing things by heart" (p. 257).

A typical example of the *Selectividad* involves two days of written examinations on subjects studied in school, but will include a session on taking notes and writing a précis from a specimen lecture, with the purpose of assessing aptitude for learning and study in higher education.

Support systems

A reform programme of this kind which is so dependent on the teachers requires an extensive provision of support structures if it is to be implemented successfully. New patterns of assessment imply changes in the initial training of teachers and in provision for in-service training, and the organisation of structures for advice, information, consultation and co-operative working among the teachers.

In initial training, courses on assessment must be given a more prominent place. A separate Plan for Teacher Training is promised, to cover development over the next six years. In in-service training and professional development of teachers, there is a promise to increase substantially the provision for seminars and courses and periods of sabbatical study. A salary increment has been agreed for teachers who have completed (over a six-year period) 100 hours of in-service training (though there is no check on how they have benefited). An even more ambitious proposal is that there should be an advisory department in each school (above a certain number of staff, unspecified), a group of teachers who will have the responsibility of helping to implement the new approaches, co-ordinating arrangements for assessment and developing the criteria for evaluation specified in the decrees, with assistance from university and college staff.

These plans will not easily be realised and they have substantial resource implications. Already in existence, however, is a country-wide network of Teachers' Centres (CEP, *Centros de Professores*), varying in size to as many as 20 staff. Their functions, recognised in the 1991 decrees, are to work with teachers in developing curricular schemes and materials, to initiate projects involving teachers and to stimulate educational research on teaching and learning. Thus, the need for support is recognised, but there are issues of cost, staffing and mode of operation which are as yet unresolved.

Issues

This review has focused on proposals for reform. Since these plans are still at the discussion stage, we must wait to see how the schools use the freedom from traditional examining and the responsibility for their own assessment. The reforms clearly have initiated a process of change: some ten years ago, the overall judgement in a review by McNair (1981) was that there had been successful progress towards greater equality of opportunity, democratic delegation of powers, new curricular objectives and the use of less formal continuous assessment in place of annual testing by traditional examinations.

Much of the discussion, however, is still at the level of statements of intent. Putting them into practice requires effort, consultation, agreement, time and funding: we are still in the early stages of the change process. It takes time to establish a consensus on objectives, especially when there are concurrently profound political changes, nationally and in the autonomous communities. Now there is a need to build mediating structures to help implement the proposals: support structures for guidance and consultation, revision of the professional education of teachers, both initial and in-service, and monitoring to evaluate the progress and effects of the reforms, to be armed with evidence against a possible backlash of professional or public opinion.

From this general review, three issues may be identified as distinctive themes: the move towards formative rather than summative assessment; the central role of teachers in assessment; and the broadening of the concept of assessment to include process strategies of learning as well as content knowledge.

The move towards formative assessment does not imply a diminution in the amount of examining, but rather a reduction in the emphasis on it as a selective instrument which characterised the traditional educational provision. Continuous, formative, school-based assessment, integrating testing with teaching and learning, means more work, not less. The change may best be described as a move towards "low stakes" examining in which assessment performs a supportive guidance function, in place of "high stakes" examinations which crucially decide pupils' educational opportunities and life chances. Nevertheless, the external pressures of competition and selection, which create the demand for "high stakes" examinations, cannot be eliminated by decree or even by extensive public consultation. Parents rightly expect to be informed about their children's achievements, often in normative terms of how their children stand in comparison with others; and public confidence in schools and teachers is built on evidence of successful attainment, which is usually in terms of knowledge and information, and predominantly normative. There is, of course, provision for full and regular reports to parents and for consultation with them on crucial decisions. There are no plans for published comparisons of results for schools or for regions, or for teacher appraisal on the basis of test results. (A proposal for linking teachers' promotion to appraisal on these lines was dropped in the face of strong professional opposition.) The pressures of external constraints are deferred by the reforms until pupils approach the age of 16, in that the hidden element of selection in the practice of *repetir curso* is greatly reduced; but the requirements of entry to higher education and employment continue to exercise their influence on the later stages, and possibly may extend that influence into earlier years.

Responsibility for assessment is placed firmly on teachers and schools. If there is public confidence in the educational provision, this can avoid the well-known unfairness of the formal examination in which so much depends on performance "on the day" or on coaching in examination technique. Critics of the proposals query the wisdom of this allocation of responsibility to teachers, doubting whether a professional body can be a force for reform rather than merely protect professional interest, whether teachers can perform this function more efficiently, more fairly and more economically than formal examinations, and whether teachers can retain the necessary public confidence in their judgements and resist private pressures without the support of an external independent national examination system.

Changes in assessment are part of an overall educational reform:

> "The legal framework of the curriculum has moved progressively in a clear direction: from the old traditional plan of studies consisting merely in mastering content... to one which aims, using knowledge, to shape pupils' skills, aptitudes, attitudes and values... The knowledge explosion and the vast growth of science and technology make it impossible to rely on traditional forms of teaching based on memorising content, rapidly obsolescent, within a closed system. Today's student needs to learn methods of learning..." (Muñoz Sedano, 1987).

Translating this high ideal into practice, and devising methods of assessment which will support the change, present a formidable challenge. The powerful claims of specialist disciplines, the extensive technical knowledge required by modern society, and popular conceptions of what is expected of education, all stand in the way of such a change. (The fact that in Spanish, one term, *evaluacion*, is used for assessment or examinations or evaluation may be instanced as an illustration of the limitations of popular understanding of the issues.) To quote one critic:

> "In the Spanish education system, there exists no tradition or knowledge of the need to use examinations and other assessment to contribute to the improvement of learning processes and the curriculum. With the new legislation, one foresees the start of a policy of diagnosis of basic output; but there are no channels for using the results which could be obtained."

Thus, what is needed is not just a new system, but a new view of the role of assessment, a change of attitude among teachers and among the public. Public and professional attitudes to assessment in education constitute an "assessment culture", which, like other cultures, rests on a common set of assumptions and beliefs and depends on familiarity with long-established practices. It is not surprising that the process of change is slow and difficult.

ACKNOWLEDGMENTS

The assistance of the following is gratefully acknowledged: Alvaro Marchesi and colleagues at the Ministry of Education and Science, in particular, Ignacio Gonzalo; Mariano Alvaro and colleagues at CIDE; Jose Gimeno Sacristan, University of Valencia; Cesar Coll Salvador, University of Barcelona; Alba Chaparro; and participants in the April 1991 Barcelona Conference, *Jornades d'Estudi*.

REFERENCES

(Unattributed references are from interviews or correspondence)

ALVARO PAGE, M. *y otros* (1988) "Evaluacion externa de la reforma experimental de las Enseñanzas Medias" *(segunda generacion)*, *Revista de Educacion,* 287, pp. 5-30.

ALVARO PAGE, M. and CERDAN VICTORIA, J. (1988), "De la evaluacion externa de la reforma de las Enseñanzas Medias a la evaluacion permanente del sistema educativo", *Revista de Educacion,* 287, pp. 181-229.

McNAIR, J. (1981), "Education in Spain, 1970-80: the years of compulsory schooling". *Comparative Education,* 17, pp. 47-57.

MUÑOZ SEDANO, A. (1987), "Analisis de la situacion espanola: la evolution del curriculum de la EGB y las estrategias de aprendizaje", In: Nisbet, J. and Shucksmith, J., *Estrategias de Aprendizaje*. Madrid: Santillana, S.J., pp. 137-166.

Real Decreto 1006/71 and 1007/91, 14 June 1991; Annexes *Boletin Oficial del Estado,* numero 152. Madrid: Ministerio de Educacion y Ciencia.

White Paper for the Reform of the Education System (1990). Madrid: Ministerio de Educacion y Ciencia.

White Paper: La Educacion en España (1969). Madrid: Ministerio de Educacion y Ciencia.

Chapter 6

SWEDEN

by
Professor Margaret Sutherland
University of Leeds

The national system

The education system of Sweden has for the latter part of this century been regarded as one of the most progressive in Western Europe, offering models of reform to other countries. It accepts two principles which have been emphasized in many educational reforms - providing equal opportunities for all and respecting the rights of the individual. It combines the desire to reduce the importance of school marks and other formal assessments with a highly organised, expert system of marking and constructing tests. It is now attempting some decentralisation in a strongly centralised system. Reconciling these various principles may be a matter of some difficulty, especially when there is growing concern with ensuring the overall quality of education from the national point of view. But as Sweden has also pioneered the technique of "rolling reform", frequent reviews of the education system can produce further attempts to remove anomalies or defects appearing in its working.

The Swedish system has been firmly centralised under the control of the National Board of Education which has been responsible for defining the curriculum and carrying out assessment of various kinds. But in 1991, to give greater autonomy to municipalities, the National Board was disbanded, being replaced by a smaller, "leaner", National Agency for Education. (A less dramatic but similar change had taken place a little earlier in the National Board for Universities and Colleges which will in future have fewer resources allocated to its work and will allow greater autonomy to the universities.) Nevertheless, a considerable amount of centralisation remains.

In Sweden a nine-year compulsory school provides comprehensive education for all children from age 7 to age 16. This school (established after various experiments in the 1950s and 1960s) is now divided into three levels -- junior, middle and senior -- each of three years' duration. It is followed by an upper secondary school which all young people who have completed the nine-year school can enter - more than 90 per cent do so. Rather less than one per cent of pupils attend private schools.

The curriculum is determined by statutory provisions defining the aims of education and the subjects to be taught. The National Board has had the responsibility for ensuring the implementation of these legal requirements, but under the new system, municipalities become responsible for achieving the goals defined by the State. The central statement of the curriculum (*Läroplan*, legally established in 1980, implemented since 1982) outlines the general purposes of education and the skills to be developed, as well as stating for each level of the school the specific aims and objectives in the teaching of each subject: it also indicates the number of hours per subject. Time is allocated to project work (within the compulsory subjects) and at middle level and senior level two or three periods per week are to be given to pupils' "free activities". Among other guiding principles are included the importance of variety in methods of teaching, of occasional vertical grouping, of adapting to individual characteristics, of creating a democratic atmosphere in the school. The curriculum is the same for all pupils except that in the senior level classes (ages 13-15) pupils have an optional course which can be a second foreign language (all pupils study English from junior level class 3, age 9, onwards). In senior level also pupils have to decide between general or more advanced courses in English and mathematics. (Pupils from immigrant families -- about 10 per cent of the school population -- have in addition the right to taught their home language.)

The curriculum for the upper secondary school is also centrally defined but a remarkable variety of "lines" is offered here for pupils' choice (subject to availability in the pupil's neighbourhood). Some 25 lines provide for teaching in six sectors -- industry and crafts; caring professions, social services and consumer education; economics, commerce and office work; languages, social sciences and the arts; technology and science; agriculture, forestry and horticulture. In all lines Swedish, civics or orientation to working life, and physical education must be included. English must be studied in the "theoretical" lines and also in some of those providing vocational subjects. The length of the courses varies: there is one four-year line (technology), others last for three years or for two - but the two-year lines are now to be extended to three years, despite some controversy as to whether they should become more general or more specifically vocational.

In an education system which has striven to develop equality between females and males, one of the astonishing aspects of student choice in the curriculum at upper secondary level is the very considerable gender bias, females opting especially for social studies, liberal arts, caring and service occupations, while males remain the great majority in technical and technological studies.

Assessment

Diagnostic

Although transition from one level to another of the compulsory school is automatic, tests are provided by the National Board for use in classes 3, 6 and 9, that is, at points of transition to a higher school level. (Some such tests are also available for use by teachers in upper secondary school vocational lines.) The purpose of these tests, which try to use simple, everyday materials and to offer questions with which about 90-95 per cent of pupils can cope, is to discover those who are not acquiring the necessary proficiency in Swedish and mathematics. Pupils whose performance on these diagnostic tests is not satisfactory are to be given extra remedial teaching.

Standardizing and selecting

In Sweden a five-point marking scale is used, with 5 being the best mark. Marks do not have to be given in the compulsory school except in classes 8 and 9: at earlier levels teachers are expected rather to keep continuous records of individual pupils' progress. The selective function of school marks has until the 1990s been important at two levels: (i) for entry into certain lines of the upper secondary school, (ii) at the end of upper secondary school, for entry into higher education. But now at the beginning of upper secondary school, although formerly a high mark level was required for entry to some lines, recruitment difficulties and a respect for democratic principles have produced the situation in which pupils are normally allowed to enter the line they choose, provided places are available. At the end of upper secondary education a change in conditions of entry for the Scholastic Aptitude Test, which was earlier intended only for adults seeking entry to higher education, has meant that upper secondary leavers can now opt to use marks obtained in this test (which will be discussed later) rather than school marks as their passport into their preferred university course.

Where selection by marks has taken place, it is perhaps a further instance of democratic openness that marks obtained by pupils taking either general or more advanced courses in maths and English in class 9 have counted equally in entry to upper secondary education: and for entry to higher education marks obtained at the end of a two-year line have been accepted on the same basis as those obtained in three-year lines, though students coming from two-year lines probably have to give an additional year to obtain specific subject qualifications for their preferred course.

Recent changes have clearly reduced the selective function of school marks. Central assessments which have served mainly to standardize school assessments are also likely to be modified in the near future.

Under the system existing until 1991/92, to make marks obtained in school classes 8 and 9 comparable from school to school, centrally produced tests of achievement in English have been given in class 8 and tests of Swedish and mathematics in class 9. These tests have been constructed by the National Board of Education in consultation with experts and reference groups of experienced teachers. The test items are tried in a number of schools and the results analysed: unreliable items are eliminated or altered to produce the final version. The test results received from the schools are analysed and standardized scales determined. Individual teachers can then know from the results of the central tests how their classes compare in achievement with classes in the rest of the country and use this information in giving marks to individual pupils within their classes. While the use of these tests is not compulsory in the nine-year school, in practice the great majority (some 80 per cent) of teachers use them. Since the same tests are used during a number of years, they are kept confidential.

In the upper secondary school the use of the centrally standardized achievement tests is compulsory. The centrally produced tests make assessments in various subjects - Swedish, mathematics, English, French, German, physics, chemistry and some vocational subjects - and they are spaced out over two years (according to the lines in question), to avoid overloading of pupils. They are constructed by teams working in university departments in the same way as tests for the nine-year school - by consultation with reference groups, item analysis and standardization - but they are new each year, so past tests are published and discussed. Within the schools, teachers have to set a required number of their own tests in their subject each year and the marks they give for this school work have to be adjusted to correspond with the class's mark in the national standardized test. The teacher's mean mark must not deviate by more than 0.2 from the class score on the standardized test. The final award of such marks is determined by discussion by the school head and the teachers concerned, with reference to class performance on the central tests and in different subjects within the school.

Since past tests are available to the public, their influence on what is taught in the schools is likely to be considerable. Direct coaching is regarded by the people responsible for constructing these tests as probably a waste of time. But the potential influence of the tests on the curriculum, their "steering value", is recognised when they are being constructed. Efforts are made to ensure that the tests do correspond to the curriculum - they must have face validity where teachers are concerned: they are also constructed to emphasize productive rather than simply reproductive responses. They attempt to encourage the development of the skills which education is intended to foster. Even so, there have been calls for the creation of criterion-referenced rather than norm-referenced tests: movement to that kind of assessment, which obviously makes new and more complicated demands on test-constructors, may take place in the near future.

Concern for realism and validity in the construction of central tests may be illustrated by the development of testing in Swedish. Until 1985 this test in Swedish consisted of writing an essay, the subject of which was announced at the beginning of the exam. It was recognised that such spur-of-the-moment writing is not the way in which people would normally set out their views. So a change was made: the subject is announced in advance: candidates have the opportunity to consult reference sources, to talk to people about it, to hear an exposition by teachers: at the end of a week, they then write their essays. Examples of different levels of success in writing are provided for teachers marking the work. The probable increase in validity resulting from the new approach is seen as fully compensating for any loss in reliability.

The use of the central tests results to standardize marks has not always been easy to establish in the schools. Teachers initially found it difficult to understand how their marks should be adjusted: some, for example, thought that a normal distribution was to be expected for each class. Conforming to the 0.2 limit of deviation may cause some teachers considerable dissatisfaction and much explanation by the headteacher may be required, though it is possible that exceptions may be allowed. The National Board of Education in fact published in 1990 a 44-page booklet on marks and marking in the upper secondary school *(Betygsättning i gymnasieskolan)*, for use by individual teachers or as material for discussion on in-service study days. This publication explains, with useful examples, the principles of testing and standardization, the use of marks in the school system and the way in which central norms should be applied.

National evaluation

Though introducing some decentralisation of control of schools, the government has at the same time been concerned as to whether the goals defined in the central curriculum are really being achieved throughout the country. While centralised tests are used to standardize assessment of various subjects in upper secondary schools and performance in Swedish, English and maths in classes 8 and 9 of the basic school, information from such sources is limited and does not cover the whole of the curriculum. Possible insights from such central tests have in fact been reduced in the last decade because standardized tests set until 1980 in class 3 (Swedish and maths), class 6 (reading, writing, English and maths) and class 8 (Swedish language and literature, writing, English, maths, German and French) were then abolished.

In Sweden, as in other countries, there is public controversy as to the merits of what is being done in schools. A further source of disquiet has been the relatively undistinguished performance of the younger age group of Swedish pupils in the second IEA maths investigation. Fuller information about actual circumstances has therefore seemed necessary to guide decision-making about methods and the curriculum in future: hence the decision to evaluate on a national basis the present implementation of the central curriculum. This evaluation was introduced in the budget proposals of 1985/86, and in a more extensive statement in 1986/87. It is noteworthy that the ministerial statement emphasized the importance of assessing not only pupils' knowledge and skills but also the other aspects of the curriculum, the methods being used, pupils' personal development and the wider activities of schools. Opinions of staff, parents and pupils were not to be overlooked.

Reports on national assessment are to be presented every three years. Consequently, a first round of national assessment was begun in 1989 when pupils in class 2 of the nine-year school were tested in reading, writing, arithmetic, art education and music, and pupils in class 5 were in Swedish, maths, English, art education, scientific and social studies. The tests for this purpose were constructed in institutions of higher education, with the guidance of a National Board steering committee. About 3 400 pupils were assessed at class 2 level and about 3 500 at class 5 level: this was a stratified random 5 per cent sample. Class 2 pupils spent 15 lesson-hours on the assessment procedures and those in class 5 spent over 20 lesson-hours. In the sample schools all classes at the relevant level were included. They responded not only to questions designed to discover their knowledge of the subjects chosen but also to questionnaires about their experience of school. Teachers and parents also answered questionnaires, the former about their work practices and the latter about their impressions of what school was providing for their children. In addition to such data came reports from earlier school visits by county education committees. In future, visits by inspectors of the National Agency will provide similar information of this kind.

Results of the first round have not yet been fully published but teachers in participating schools have received reports on their classes' performance relative to the national sample. Further useful results have, for example, been insights into teachers' various practices in setting homework or informal class tests, and indications of the need for improved in-service assistance to teachers of English in class 5.

School unit descriptions	Parent questionnaire

Total sample (9000 pupils)
Pupil questionnaire 1 (non-cognitive goals)
Pupil questionnaire 2 (opinions about schools: facts)
Pupil questionnaire 3 (opinions about schools: values)   2 lessons
Teacher questionnaire

Tests of basic knowledge in Swedish, English and Mathematics
Pupil and teacher questionnaires in Swedish, English and Mathematics
                                                              5 lessons

Subsample 1 (3000 pupils)		Subsample 2 (3000 pupils)		Subsample 3 (3000 pupils)		
(1500 pupils) Problem-solving test (omnibus) 8 lessons	(1500 pupils) Process-studies in home economics 8 lessons	Science Pupil and teacher questionnaire 4 lessons		Social subjects Pupil and teacher questionnaire 1 lesson		
		(1500 pupils) Swedish 2 lessons	(1500 pupils) English 2 lessons	Subtests in social subjects (750 pupils each) 1 2 3 4 3 lessons each		
		Arts Pupil and teacher questionnaire 2 lessons		(1000 pupils) Maths Pupil q're	(1000 pupils) Music Pupil and teacher q're	(1000 pupils) Handicraft Home Economics Physical Education Pupil and teacher q're
				3 lessons each		

Figure 4 Sweden: Assessment of knowledge, skills and attitudes in Grade 9, Spring 1992

For the second round of this evaluation (1992) work has been going on during the intervening years to prepare the assessment materials. Differences will be made in procedure. The assessment will focus mainly on class 9 (the last year of compulsory school) where about 10 per cent of the school population will be sampled. In classes 2 and 5, a 3 per cent sample will be taken, with some repetition of questions set in the first round. By a matrix sampling design of a fairly complex nature (see Figure 4) it is hoped to avoid excessive loads on any one group of pupils, though there might be a problem arising from national evaluation tests coming at the same time as the standardizing maths test for class 9. The results of the national evaluation, as in the first round, are intended to give information about group levels of performance. Their presentation at national level will not identify classes or schools, though individual teachers will again be informed about their classes' relative performance.

Since the evaluation is expected to give insight into all aspects of the curriculum, questionnaires to pupils, teachers and parents deal with some non-cognitive aspects and supplementary information is to come from school visits and observations. In the cognitive assessments, particular care is being taken to avoid concentrating simply on reproduction of factual knowledge: items are to provide information on skills and processes also. Thus, for instance, groups of pupils may be given a week in which to study a question on the condition of the environment, to consult references and people, to seek guidance from teachers, then to present, as their test performance, a report of their findings, using whatever techniques they think appropriate (graphics, videos, etc.). The teachers here have the function of being resource persons but they have also, especially, the duty of observing and assessing the way in which the groups of pupils set about their given task. Teachers must restrain their professional drive to teach: they must also be clear that this is not an assessment of individual pupils or of competition between schools: it is to produce a picture of school work in relation to the requirements of the national curriculum.

Similarly in science testing, situations which will effectively discover skills as well as knowledge are being advised, on lines rather similar to those developed in England.

It is regarded as beneficial that now some subjects which were earlier omitted from testing are being included - for example handicrafts and physical education. This inclusion may be perceived as giving these subjects enhanced status, putting them on a par with the more traditionally academic subjects. Devising suitable ways of assessing pupils' work in these subjects, or in others such as music or art appreciation, presents a valuable challenge, especially to the expert teachers consulted in test construction.

An interesting technical point is decision-making about the facility level of items chosen for national evaluation tests. It is felt that the tests should offer some challenge to the pupils but at the same time be within the capacity of the majority. In the absence of central criteria, the choice of facility level of test items could in some instances enable test-makers to influence the kind of impression the evaluation tests will give.

Entry to higher education

As has been noted, marks given in the various subjects in upper secondary schools are standardized on the basis of results in the central achievement tests: in three-year lines English, German or French, chemistry and physics are tested in the second year and mathematics and Swedish are tested in the third year. The average mark awarded, for the country as a whole, should be 3 -- the midpoint of the scale; the normative distribution of marks is: 7 per cent at each extreme (marks of 1 and 5), 24 per cent in the intermediate bands (marks of 2 and 4) and 38 per cent in the central band (a mark of 3). There may, however, be some deviations from the proposed distribution because of differences of ability in students in different lines -- there is differential recruitment to some subjects; there is also the problem of drop-outs, usually weaker students, and the consequent question of the extent to which the marks of the rest of the group should be adjusted to conform to the expected distribution.

Since 1988/89, experiments have been carried out in some vocational lines using a modular system where students receive a simple pass/fail rating on each module of study. In such cases, the students' marks for selection purposes can be based only on the marks obtained in the general subjects they also study -- English, Swedish, mathematics and civics. But this scarcely seems a satisfactory solution of the problem, especially as the modular system has been intended to improve the standing of vocational subjects.

For these and other reasons, the Scholastic Aptitude Test, or more precisely the Higher Education Test *(Högskoleprovet)*, has been given new prominence. (The recognised resemblance to the American test makes the use of the same name acceptable -- but possibly confusing.) This test was introduced at the time of Sweden's radical reform of higher education, with the intention of facilitating the entry to university studies of adults who lacked formal qualifications. Underlying the reforms was the principle enunciated in the U68 report, that higher education should not be thought of as always "end-on" to upper secondary education, catering essentially for people in the 19-24 age group, but that there should be different patterns of study and work, some people interposing a number of years in employment between their years of full-time study, others alternating study and work or engaging in part-time employment and study. The so-called 25/4 policy in Sweden has meant that adults aged 25 who have been in employment for at least four years can enter higher education - though unrestricted entry is into certain study programmes only. For longer-term courses giving a professional training, a *numerus clausus* remains and test results or schools marks decide whether students can have a place on them. The proportions of students admitted on the basis of school marks and on the basis of the Higher Education Test performance have varied from time to time, but at least one-third of students must be admitted on each criterion: the present percentages are about 60 on school results (quotas within this depending on the number of applicants from a given line) and 40 on the test.

Until 1991, the test could not be taken immediately by school-leavers; and they could, after a year, make only one attempt at it. But from 1991 onwards, pupils can attempt the Higher Education Test after the second year in upper secondary school and can attempt it four times, using their best result. The numbers of those taking the test have increased dramatically and the majority of candidates are now under the age of 21 whereas in the 1980s the majority of candidates were in the 25-29 and 30-39 age groups. Research on the test in 1990 has already indicated that there is a high correlation between marks in school exams and marks on the test, and that there is also a correlation between lines in upper secondary education and test results. The question must arise whether this new competition from younger people is going to affect the entry of mature students into higher education.

The test itself is held twice each year. The construction of items for the six sub-tests is carried out by a team working under the leadership of a university professor and goes through the various stages of item construction, discussion and revision, trial runs, data analysis, expert consultation, storage in an item bank. (It has been estimated that some 50 experts have been involved in the whole processing.) The tests are published, so they have to be new each time, and there has been some interest in coaching for the test, though again it is believed by the responsible authorities that this is unlikely to be effective. The six sub-tests, with time limits ranging from 15 to 50 minutes, are in multiple-choice form: answers are entered on answer sheets for ease of marking, and each sub-test is preceded by an illustrative example. Candidates are allowed to keep the question booklet and receive a list of correct answers after the test - if they also circle their answers on the question book they can discover how many were right. (The answer booklet also bears the words "*Lycka till!*" - good luck!).

The sub-tests are:

i) vocabulary (ORD), including both Swedish and foreign words drawn from a variety of sources;
ii) quantitative reasoning (NOG) - given a question relating to quantities, candidates have to judge which, if any, of the following statements contains the answer;
iii) reading comprehension (LäS) - candidates have to choose the correct answers to questions relating to two or more quite lengthy texts in different registers;
iv) interpretation of diagrams, charts, tables (DTK) - but this is likely to be replaced in future by a reading comprehension test in English;
v) general knowledge (AO - *allmän orientering*), with questions on a wide variety of topics such as music, sport, economics, the arts, physiology, social studies;
vi) study skills (STUF) - here students are given a work-book which is some 70 pages long and contains a number of texts: they are presented with questions to which the answers are provided somewhere in this book but as they have not enough time to read it thoroughly, they must therefore show their ability to find information by the use of the index or table of contents.

The total number of questions is 44: one mark is given for each right answer. The distribution of marks is then analysed and reduced to a twenty-one point scale of standardized scores expressed, oddly enough, in the range from 0.0 to 2.0. The mean score was, in 1990 for example, 1.01, with a median of 1.05 and a standard deviation of 0.45. These scores then serve to determine candidates' success in entering the university course they prefer, though some additional credit may be given for a number of years of work experience.

Popular response to the test has been good. Students and the general public judge it to be fair and reasonable though some educationists are concerned that it gives results from testing on one occasion only -- they would probably prefer a combination of school exam and higher education test results.

Careful analysis has been made of the results of testing in earlier years. The reliability of the sub-tests in a recent year fluctuated from 0.66 to 0.87 and the overall reliability in different years was 0.93 to 0.95. The test's predictive validity is hard to measure since university work is affected by many variables and some of it is assessed only on a pass/fail basis. One piece of research on teacher education found a higher correlation between school marks and subject success than between the Higher Education Test and subsequent success. There have also been some findings -- similar to some USA reports - that men do better than women on this test (mainly through NOG and DTK), while women tend to do better on school marks, though this latter difference depends on the line from which students come.

Issues

Sweden has made remarkable progress since the 1960s in transforming its education system and attempting to provide equal educational opportunities for all. While some social class differences remain, and social class is still found to correlate with success in education, some research evidence suggests that the relationship between the two is less in Sweden than in other Western European countries.

During this period of advance, Sweden has benefited from a strong central agency in education which has attempted to ensure equal standards in assessment and to foster the implementation of the central curriculum. Assessment has to some extent been deliberately used to influence the development of teaching methods and the content of what is taught. Assessment has also been carried out in an admirably scientific way, bringing a great deal of expertise to the construction of test items and the analysis of the data they provide. It is of particular interest that assessment procedures in various cases have emphasized realism and indicated willingness to sacrifice some degree of reliability in pursuit of greater validity.

So far as national evaluation is concerned, it is striking that there is such explicit determination to include all aspects of schools' work, giving a place to non-cognitive factors, studying not only the outcomes but also the processes of teaching. The purpose of achieving a holistic picture of education in the schools is admirable -- and ambitious. The collation and synthesising of data of different kinds from different sources will be no easy task. Carrying out such evaluations at three-yearly intervals is also admirable. At the same time it has to be recognised that test construction of this kind is a lengthy process, taking at least two years: this is therefore not an instrument which can be rapidly modified according to changes in political will or to changes in the questions set by governments.

A further question remains -- though it may be answered as evaluation results are published -- as to whether this central assessment is the best method of discovering the characteristics of the work being done in schools. Certainly attempts are being made to disrupt the work of individuals as little as possible and evaluative instruments are being carefully created. But possibly other approaches -- for instance, a combination of the views of inspectors, parents' organisations and professional associations of teachers -- could provide as useful information. The other important question is how results are to be used. Some outcomes of a valuable kind have already been noted; but methods of remedying any great deficiencies in individual schools have still to be defined.

The National Board of Education has clearly exercised its various responsibilities for assessment most efficiently and intelligently. At the same time, the very strength of the National Board may have had the weakness of encouraging a receptive, passive attitude on the part of teachers. Although very great care has been taken to ensure that groups of teachers are involved in test production, and in discussions of the whole trend and contents of tests, teachers at the upper level of the nine-year school and in upper secondary classes must find themselves constrained in adjusting their marking to the national norms -- even though it is also helpful to teachers to know how their classes' performance compares with that of classes elsewhere. There have certainly been difficulties in the past in making clear to teachers the use to be made of the centralised tests. It is also a curious phenomenon that, although there are limits to deviation from the national mean, the national statistics show an upward drift to means of 3.2 or even 3.4 in some subjects.

The movement towards the abolition of formal school marks as a discriminating and selective instrument might well encourage similar changes in other education systems. What could be described as the primary school classes have been freed from such assessments: in junior secondary years, the selective function is almost gone as admission to upper secondary lines has come to depend almost entirely on pupil choice. The traditional "final examination" of Swedish academic secondary schools, leading to successful candidates' matriculation qualification and the right to wear the cherished "student's cap", has been superseded for many years now by the less dramatic accumulation of marks obtained over a period of time in the upper secondary lines; and even this remaining selective function of school education has been diminished as the alternative assessment for entry to some higher education courses becomes more widely used -- though it is still uncertain whether a Scholastic Aptitude Test will be a fully satisfactory substitute. (It may also be noted in passing that selection for some forms of higher education seems unavoidable.) In these circumstances, the need for central assessments to standardize marks at secondary school level would seem to be diminishing to vanishing point. At the same time, the apparent uncertainty of the government as to what the work of the schools is achieving would seem to reinforce the need for some kind of alternative assessment.

Diagnostic tests of course may well continue to be of value to teachers at the various levels of the nine-year school, to focus on deficiencies in some pupils' progress more sharply than teachers' continuous assessment may do. Other consequences of the elimination of selective marks and standardized assessments must be considered, especially those affecting the curriculum and the teachers. At present, some teachers do use past test papers as the basis of teaching, although the more enlightened use them simply to acquaint their pupils with the form of the test. Nevertheless, the central test papers from year to year serve to signal to the schools both what subject content is important and what processes and skills are to be developed. Their construction is carried out in the awareness of this "steering function". Their elimination, or reduction in importance, would need to be accompanied by other methods of communication with teachers, possibly by greater reliance on their professional judgement and better communication within the teaching profession. Such developments might also serve to give to teachers useful information, at present supplied by central tests, about their pupils' performance compared to the national average. The successive stages of the national evaluation admittedly will give some teachers some such information, but all teachers can profit by some standards for comparison.

Alternatively, there has been considerable discussion in recent decades of the need to replace the norm-referenced upper secondary school tests by criterion-referenced tests. For a variety of reasons, including the additional difficulties of devising such tests - criterion-referencing is not a straightforward process - the proposals for this change have not been implemented. The form of the central tests will change from 1992 onwards. If indeed they move to criterion-referencing they can well serve the new purpose of certification of achievement on completion of upper secondary education as well as offer valuable guidance to teachers.

The curriculum at present remains enshrined in a central statement, though it is to be reviewed in the first half of the present decade. Plans for continuing national evaluation seem to indicate the determination to maintain a central curriculum, though the holistic view of the schools' work may well indicate whether changes of emphasis, or greater or less flexibility in the centralised statement, are needed. Again, the question of the amount and kind of centralisation required in a unit of Sweden's size remains open.

Sweden has exemplified the highly sophisticated use of various forms of assessment in a system whose guiding principles are against producing feelings of inequality or closing access to different levels of education. There seems to be a general acceptance of the view that great progress has been made towards such equality of educational provision throughout the country (the problem of immigrant children has perhaps been less acute in Sweden than in some other parts of Europe). Yet problems, criticisms and uncertainties about what the schools are achieving remain within the country. Whether improvement will come best through different and improved assessments and evaluations or through abandonment of centralised norms and central control remains a fascinating question.

REFERENCES

Gymnasieavdelningen, Sö (1990), *Betygsättning i gymnasieskolan.* Stockholm: Skolöverstyrelsen.

National Board of Education (1986), "The Swedish School System: Fact Sheets." Stockholm: Swedish National Board of Education, Information Section.

National Board of Education (1990), "National Evaluation of Swedish Schools and Adult Education". NBE Information, 1 90:4.

National Board of Education (1990), "Examinations and Marking Systems in Swedish Upper Secondary Schools." NBE Information, 1 90:13.

UHä, Studerandeavdelningen (1991), *Antagning på prov: Fakta om högskoleprovet.* Stockholm: UHä.

UHä (1990) *Högskoleprovet 1991. Provexempel och information till prövande.* Stockholm: UHä.

Chapter 7

THE UNITED KINGDOM

by
Doctor Caroline Gipps
University of London Institute of Education

England and Wales, Northern Ireland and Scotland have separate education systems. This review focuses on developments in England and Scotland, with brief references to Wales and Northern Ireland.

England and Wales

In England and Wales in recent years, various new developments in assessment have attempted to integrate assessment with learning, to widen the method of assessment, to enable more pupils to achieve success and to reduce the role of the end-of-course examination. In 1988, the new national curriculum and assessment programme was introduced which was to overtake the new developments and to provide, within one programme, assessment which would support learning and measure performance for accountability and selection purposes -- a kind of high stakes "authentic" or "performance" assessment. However, the first round of assessment was problematic: the criterion-referenced assessment activities were impractical for surveying the whole age group, and did not offer sufficient comparability for evaluative purposes. As a result, the government has announced its intention to pull back from this new style of assessment and return to a more traditional model of testing. This chapter gives a detailed account of the developments and discusses some of the reasons for this shift.

National testing in England and Wales

The Education Reform Act (ERA) of 1988 brought about wide-ranging changes in education in England and Wales. (Comparable changes were introduced in Scotland and Northern Ireland: these are reviewed later.) A major strand of this reform was the implementation of a national curriculum and national assessment programme. The Conservative government under Margaret Thatcher intended fundamentally to restructure the education system and improve the quality and availability of appropriate education in order to help overcome Great Britain's economic problems.

At the heart of these developments was a concern about educational standards in terms of the range of curriculum experiences offered to pupils in different schools, the rigour of teaching in the basic skills, and low expectations for pupil performance. The first and last of these three had been a regularly voiced criticism by the independent Her Majesty's Inspectorate (HMI) in England and Wales. In reality there is less curricular variation at secondary level than at primary level since the upper secondary school curriculum is to a great extent controlled by the public or school-leaving exams at 16 and 18. The concerns at secondary level were more that pupils were dropping subjects, in order to specialise, as young as 13 or 14 and that the range of curricular provision for the bottom 40 per cent of the ability range was inadequate.

There were no formal assessments in the system before the public examination at 16: there is no leaving examination or certificate on leaving primary school (11+) although use of standardized tests of reading and mathematics is widespread at this stage.

The national curriculum was therefore designed to ensure that all pupils of compulsory school age (5-16) would follow the same course with English, mathematics and science forming the core, and history, geography, technology, a modern foreign language, art, music and physical education -- the foundation subjects -- forming an extended core. These ten subjects together should make up 70 per cent of curriculum time.

For each subject the curriculum is enshrined in law: statutory orders describe the matters, skills and processes to be taught as "programmes of study" and the knowledge, skills and understanding as "attainment targets" which pupils are expected to have reached at certain stages of schooling. The stages are defined as Key Stage One (5-7), Two (7-11), Three (11-14) and Four (14-16).

The national assessment programme is a crucial accompaniment to the national curriculum for it is through the assessment programme that standards are to be raised. Although the Department of Education and Science (DES) maintain that it is not an assessment-led curriculum, some observers see the national curriculum as a crude framework for the testing programme. It is in any case true that the first stage of the development of the national curriculum and assessment programme was the setting up of the Task Group on Assessment and Testing (TGAT). The report of this group (DES, 1988) put forward a blue-print for the structure of the curriculum to which all subjects had to adhere. Subjects are divided up into a number of components and within these the attainment targets are articulated at a series of ten levels. The series of levels is designed to enable progression: most pupils of 7+ would be at level two in the system while most pupils of 11+ would be at level four and so on. The attainment targets are articulated at each of the ten levels by a series of criteria or statements of attainment which form the basic structure of a criterion-referenced assessment system.

The underlying model of national curriculum and assessment is therefore an objectives model of the curriculum (embodied in the attainment targets and statements of attainment) with an encouragement for teachers to focus on skills and processes (the programmes of study) linked to a criterion-referenced assessment system.

A significant factor in the call for an improvement in educational standards was a report published in 1983 comparing performance in mathematics standards in schools in England and West Germany. The authors re-worked data from the 1964 International Evaluation of Achievement Study and claimed that German pupils in the bottom half of the ability range obtained levels of performance comparable with the average for the whole ability range in England (Prais and Wagner, 1983).

A number of other international comparisons also showed that English schools were not top of the league tables. The previous national assessment programme, the Assessment of Performance Unit (APU) which had carried out anonymous testing of "light" samples of pupils, had been unable to comment satisfactorily (because of measurement problems) on whether national standards were rising or falling. These other studies shifted the argument away from comparisons over time to comparisons of English schools with those of other countries: politically a more powerful argument within the context of the discussions about economic decline.

The National Assessment Programme in England

The national assessment programme, as outlined in the TGAT report and the statutory orders, requires that pupils be assessed against the attainment targets by their teachers continuously and by external tests (called standard assessment tasks) at the ages of 7, 11, 14 and 16. At these ages the results of teacher assessment (TA) and the external tests (SATs) are combined and must be reported towards the end of that school year. The results of individual pupils are confidential to themselves, their parents and teachers; results for a class as a whole and a school as a whole are to be available to the parents; results at school level are to be publicly reported at 11, 14 and 16; publication of results at 7 is not mandatory but is strongly encouraged by the Secretary of State. The publication of results is to be part of a broader report by the school of its work as a whole; the TGAT report suggested that such reports should include a general report for the area "to indicate the nature of socio-economic and other influences which are known to affect schools". At 16 the external test is to be the General Certificate of Secondary Education (GCSE) which is currently taken by approximately 85 per cent of the age group, and the grading system of the GCSE is to be merged with the ten-level national curriculum scale.

The national assessment proposals for Wales are similar to those for England except that Welsh is assessed as a first language and as a second language. SATs are available in both English and Welsh. In Welsh medium schools, pupils are assessed on maths, science and Welsh at 7, and these subjects together with English at 11.

The first run of assessment for 7-year-olds in English, maths and science took place in 1991, the first statutory run for 14-year-olds will be in 1993, for 11-year-olds in 1994 and in that year also GCSE will be reported in line with attainment targets and national curriculum levels. Subjects beyond the core will come on stream and be assessed in later years, with technology being the first (1992 for 7-year-olds using a non-statutory SAT, 1993 for 14-year-olds, 1994 for 11 and 1995 for 16-year-olds). All subjects should be included in the assessment programme at all ages by 1997, though teacher assessment is likely to dominate beyond the core subjects, rather than SATs.

While the overall plan for national assessment is the same for all four ages, there are differences in articulation: national assessment at 16 is dominated by the demands of GCSE; the assessments for 11-year-olds are not yet at the blue print stage; the 14-year-old assessments have been trialled in 1991 and will be piloted in 1992; while it is the assessment of 7-year-olds which is furthest along the path of development. The detailed account of the national assessment programme which follows is therefore based on the developments thus far in the assessment of 7-year-olds. The issues which are raised are, however, relevant to the whole programme.

During the spring term (to be extended to include the early summer term) of the year in which pupils reach the age of seven (Year 2), teachers make an assessment of each pupil's level of attainment on levels 1-4 of the scale 1-10 in relation to the attainment targets of the core subjects. Teachers may make these assessments in any way they wish, but observation, regular informal assessment and keeping examples of work, are all encouraged. In the first half of the summer term (to be extended to include the second half of the Spring term) the pupils are given, by their teacher, a series of standard assessment tasks (SATs) covering a sample of the core attainment targets.

Because of the reliance on teacher assessment, the TGAT report suggested a complex process of group moderation through which teachers' assessments could be brought into line around a common standard. The combination of TA and SAT results has been a contentious area; the ruling is that where an attainment target is assessed by both TA and SAT and the results differ, the SAT result is to be "preferred". If the teacher does not agree with this for an individual pupil, he/she may appeal if the SAT result would alter the overall level for the profile component (a group of attainment targets). Since the number of attainment targets assessed by SATs in maths and science is low (3/14 and 2/17 respectively), appeals are unlikely in these subjects since TA will be the dominant mode of assessment and the SAT results will have little effect. For English, all the attainment targets are assessed by SAT except for listening and speaking and, therefore, the SAT will have more impact.

Since the proposals for the SATs in the TGAT report were innovatory and were a conscious attempt to move away from traditional standardized procedures, they will be described in some detail. The TGAT report suggested that a mixture of instruments including tests, practical tasks and observations be used in order to minimise curriculum distortion and that a broad range of assessment instruments sampling a broad range of attainment targets would discourage the narrowing tendency to teach to the test. Thus, the TGAT model was one which emphasized a wide range of assessment tasks involving a wide range of response modes in order to minimise the negative effects normally associated with formal assessment.

The report addressed overburdening both teachers and children at age 7 and considered whether only the core subjects should be assessed. It rejected this proposition because it could have the effect of narrowing the primary curriculum to an undesirable extent. Mindful of the anxiety about the formal assessment of young children, the report made a number of suggestions: that the number of SATs be limited to three; that they should not be differentiated but open-ended so that all children take the same task and perform at different levels; and the SATs should be selected by the teacher from item banks. The model thus envisaged a choice of SAT so that they relate to the children's experience and a range of assessments in different contexts to ensure validity.

Early on in the development of the SATs for Key Stage One, the requirement was that they should cover as many attainment targets (AT) as possible. This proved unwieldy since there are 32 ATs in the original curriculum structure for the core and the mode of assessment was to be active rather than paper-and-pencil tests of the traditional standardized type.

In the event, the SATs used with 7-year-olds in 1991 were a watered down version of the TGAT proposals. They were differentiated, there was no choice of SAT task within attainment targets, although there was a constrained choice across ATs for science and maths. The style of assessment was however active and similar to good infant school practice: for example, the reading task at level two involved reading aloud a short passage from a children's book chosen from a list of popular titles, using dice to play maths "games", using objects to sort, etc.

As for standardization in administration of the SATs, the most important consideration is that pupils should understand what is expected of them. Thus, there is no restriction on which is said or on the use of the skills of another adult who is normally present in the classroom. There is no restriction on non-linguistic methods of presentation, there is no limit on pupils working in whatever language or combination of languages they normally use in mathematics or science. However, pupils are not allowed to explain tasks to each other nor may children whose mother tongue is not English have the English tasks explained to them in their mother tongue.

Despite the reduction in the number of ATs tested from 32 to 9, the SAT administration took a minimum of 40 hours for a class of 25-30 and was rarely managed without support for the class teacher, since most of the SATs were done with groups of four pupils. The SATs can thus be seen as matching good teaching practice, providing teachers with detailed information about individual children, but being time-consuming and offering limited standardization for comparability purposes.

In response to the widespread publicity about the amount of time the 7-year-old SATs were taking, the Prime Minister announced in the summer of 1991 that for 1992 there will be a move to shorter standardized paper-and-pencil tests. Similarly, the trialling of SATs for 14-year-olds which took place in 1991 involved extended tasks taking many hours of classroom time and covering a range of activities and response modes. The Secretary of State for Education has deemed this inappropriate, and the pilot SATs in 1992 must be short written tests done by whole classes at the same time under examination conditions. Practical tests should only be set where there is no alternative and should take only one lesson. The tests for 11-year-olds are now likely to follow the model of the 14-year-old assessments rather than the SATs envisaged in the TGAT report.

Thus, attempts to move towards a new model of assessment within national assessment are being thwarted. The reasons for this and the implications will be discussed in the section on "Issues".

Northern Ireland

The proposals put forward by the Northern Ireland Schools Examination and Assessment Council (NISEAC) in early 1991 differed from the proposals for England and Wales in a number of significant ways. There were to be no external tests: rather, assessment was to be by continuous teacher assessment, but "external assessment resources" would be available for teachers to use as part of this process. Secondly, it was not proposed that each pupil be assessed on the ten levels in relation to every AT, rather that individual performance be reported in relation to the subject. There was no mention of the publication of group results and thus accountability and raising standards were not to the fore. However, the Minister's response to the NISEAC proposals brings the Northern Ireland system much more into line with the English system: there will be external tests at 8, 11, 14 and 16; they will provide a level of attainment for each AT in each subject tested; aggregation rules will be developed to provide a level of attainment in each subject; and summaries of school results will be required (though this is only an "encouragement" at age 8).

Public examinations in England and Wales

The General Certificate of Secondary Education (GCSE) is the public examination taken by pupils at 16+. This is itself a relatively new examination with the first papers taken in 1988. The changes which were brought in with GCSE were: use of coursework assessment rather than 100 per cent examination, thus oral, practical and extended project work play an important part in the assessment; it is aimed at the whole ability range; differentiated exam papers (pitched at different levels) are therefore required for some subjects; it was intended to be criterion-referenced so that candidates could be graded in relation to their own performance rather than in relation to how others performed.

The GCSE has, it is generally acknowledged, brought about changes in teaching style and content resulting in a broadening of students' curricular and school experience. A higher proportion of the age group takes it than was the case with the previous 16+ exams (over 85 per cent of the age group enter at least one subject). Coursework assessment has had a powerful effect in many schools; 100 per cent coursework-assessed syllabuses are popular in English and are available in a number of other subjects. The move towards criterion-referencing has been problematic and pupils are graded on the basis of rather loose grade descriptions while the proportions achieving each grade were held roughly constant in the first two years in line with the previous public examination. Since the announcement of the national assessment proposals, the search for better criterion-referencing for GCSE has been halted.

Ironically, one of the justifications for making GSCE criterion-referenced was that it would help to raise standards: since there would be no limit on the number of pupils able to gain top grades, this would encourage teachers and pupils to aim, and achieve, higher. The percentage of the age group gaining the top three grades has in fact risen, with the result that there are claims now being made that the exam is too easy. The Prime Minister said in the summer of 1991 that the GCSE must be "properly calibrated to challenge the most able". Coursework assessment is also seen by the administration as being not sufficiently rigorous and too dependent on teachers. At the beginning of 1991 the Prime Minister therefore announced that all GCSEs must have some final examination; by the summer he announced that for most subjects a maximum of 20 per cent of the marks should be awarded for coursework.

Since the introduction of the national curriculum into schools, two changes have been announced to it which have resulted directly from the difficulties of aligning the GCSE with the national curriculum and assessment programme. The government's intention is to retain GCSE as the standards flagship and it is not prepared for a weakening or watering-down of its requirements. Since each GCSE course requires 10 per cent of curriculum time (for the two years from 14-16) it is clear that not all students could follow a GCSE course in all ten national curriculum subjects (plus religious education) since this would in theory leave no time for other non-statutory aspects of the curriculum (for example classics, a second foreign language, personal, social and health education, etc.). At the beginning of 1991 the Secretary of State for Education thus announced that the full national curriculum would only be followed up to the age of 14. From 14-16 all pupils must follow a full GCSE course in the core subjects (English, mathematics and science); all pupils must study technology and a modern foreign language but not necessarily to GCSE level; all pupils must follow a course of either history or geography or half of each; only a full course will be examined by GCSE. Art and music will be optional at this stage as will physical education, although schools are expected to encourage all pupils to continue with some form of the latter. Subjects which are not assessed via the GCSE (all except the core) may be assessed via examinations developed by the vocational examining bodies. The expectation is that more able pupils will take GCSEs while less able pupils will go for the vocational qualifications. Thus, the notion of a full entitlement curriculum for all, offering a broad general education to 16, has been watered down. The "option" system at 14 will be similar to that already operating in many schools, and an academic/vocational divide is built in. (That said, all pupils must continue with a full course of science and some technology to 16.)

The second major change to come about is a restructuring of the maths and science curricula. The original national curriculum structure gave maths 14 attainment targets and science 17. The examining bodies which are responsible for producing, selling, marking and analysing the GCSE announced that they could not report performance on the ten-level scale in relation to this attainment target structure. As a result, both curricula have been streamlined to five (broader) attainment targets with approximately half the number of statements of attainment, while the programmes of study remain largely unchanged. This new structure should therefore not affect teaching plans but will make the assessment simpler for both teachers and examining bodies.

It is a clear indication of the perceived importance of the GCSE that its requirements were allowed to modify the national curriculum and assessment programme in this way rather than vice versa. In addition, the return towards the domination of the formal written examination mirrors developments in relation to the SATs. This will be discussed further in the section on "Issues".

The public examination for 18-year-olds, the General Certificate of Education: Advanced Level (GCE "A" level), is traditionally seen as an exam for the elite of the age group who are aiming for higher education : 20 per cent of the age group enter the examination (of those who start the course 10 per cent drop out) and 20 per cent of these fail. Attempts to reform A level, to broaden it and to encourage the development of high-status vocational qualifications for this age group, have been on the educational agenda for some time. The current "AS level" exam -- equivalent to half an A level in study time but of the same "depth" or "standard" -- is an attempt to encourage students to study more subjects than the usual two or three; it is, however, still aimed at the same population of students.

A recent White Paper outlines the government's plans for 16-19 education and training (DES, 1991). A and AS levels and the standards they maintain are to remain. The syllabuses need to evolve but without undermining the consistency of high standards. In order to do this, there will be a framework to control syllabuses (as there is with GCSE) from September 1994. As with GCSE, a maximum of 20 per cent coursework assessment will be allowed. The main thrust of the paper, however, is with the new vocational qualifications which are to be developed "as fast as possible" so that a comprehensive framework of general national vocational qualifications is in place by the end of 1992. The style of these new assessments is not yet clear, but performance is to be reported in relation to five levels of competence. The levels within this accreditation framework will relate thus: Level 1 to National Curriculum; Level 2 to GCSE; Level 3 to A/AS level; Level 4 to degree level; Level 5 to post-graduate qualification level. This development will extend the range of vocational qualifications currently offered by the National Council for Vocational Qualifications (NCVQ), the Business and Technician Education Council (BTEC) and the Certificate of Pre-Vocational Education (CPVE). An important theme of the paper is the need to ensure that these vocational qualifications have parity of esteem with the academic A and AS levels. In order to achieve this, both types of courses will be available in schools and colleges and a system of diplomas is to be introduced which will be awarded on the basis of academic and/or vocational qualifications.

The early reactions to these suggestions have been mixed, some concern being voiced that the proposals are not sufficiently radical, that the A and AS level examining will still cream off the elite, thus continuing the academic/vocational divide which is a feature of the system in the United Kingdom. Proposals for a Technological Baccalaureate are being developed, with a pilot scheme starting in September 1991, offering students the choice of studying for either A levels or vocational qualifications within an overall technological curriculum. However, such a rethinking of the 16-19 curriculum at a national level seems unlikely at the moment.

Scotland: national testing

The situation in Scotland is rather different from that in England. The 1989 Self-Governing Schools Act (Scotland) did not bring in explicit legislation for a national curriculum and assessment programme. It simply enabled the introduction of regulations for testing in primary schools (ages 5-12). Initially, therefore, the government undertook its developments without explicit legislation but with the introduction of guidelines for education from age 5 to 14 drawn up by the Scottish Consultative Committee on the Curriculum. Following the reluctance of a substantial proportion of local authorities to support either the piloting or the implementation of the external tests, legislation was enacted by bringing in regulations in November 1990 requiring local authorities to undertake the testing.

National tests are part of the overall assessment strategy. The tests are to apply only to Primary 4 and Primary 7 (8 and 12 years of age) and will be limited to English language (reading and writing only) and mathematics. They are seen as additional to teachers' own assessments and as:

> "an important source of evidence of pupil attainment in key aspects of language and mathematics. They will tell teachers and parents about the achievement of individual pupils in relation to nationally agreed and understood standards, which teachers can use to check their own assessments and which ensure consistent interpretation by teachers of what particular levels of attainment mean."

The development and administration of the tests is in the hands of a new Primary Assessment Unit at the Scottish Examination Board. The generation of test items was carried out by working parties of teachers together with inspectors, academics and others.

Tests (except in mathematics) are made up of units containing items relating to one curriculum strand at a specified level (for example a unit on reading narrative at Level C). A catalogue of units is provided from which schools choose the tests they use. The choice of units offered to teachers clearly gives them the opportunity to incorporate the tests more naturally into their own teaching programme so that teaching to the tests will be more beneficial than is teaching to traditional standardized tests. The tests could, if properly used, turn out to fulfil a valuable formative assessment function. The flexibility apparent for promoting good teaching, however, will not serve well the other purpose of checking pupils' performance against nationally agreed and understood standards.

Judgements about the level of test chosen for each pupil will be based on the teachers' own assessments; where a pupil's level of attainment is in some doubt, tests at two levels can be taken. Thus, in Scotland teachers choose at which level to assess pupils, while in England the pupil is entered at the level deemed appropriate by the teacher, but must be given the next level up if he/she passes at the level entered. As in England, the five levels of attainment are progressive but they are labelled A to E and described (in some subjects) thus: "should be attainable by some or most pupils at stage Primary X".

Teachers will have responsibility for all the assessment on environmental studies, expressive arts and religious and moral education, and for listening and talking in language. Their assessment complements the national testing in mathematics and in the reading and writing aspects of language. The major part of what is reported to parents and School Boards, therefore, will reflect teacher assessments rather than external tests.

Information on the results has to be communicated to the Primary Assessment Unit of the Scottish Examination Board, to parents and, in summary form, to the School Board (the Scottish equivalent of the school governors in England). A distinctive feature of the Scottish scheme, however, is that comparisons among schools are not required and the government has explicitly discouraged rank ordering of pupils or use of the results for their selection for particular schools. There is thus a conscious attempt to "lower the stakes".

Reporting on individual pupils' attainments is confidential among teacher, pupil and parent. As yet, there is no clear prescription for how a summary of teacher assessments and test results should be put together, nor how variations in performance across strands within outcomes should be aggregated: a Committee on Reporting will advise on this. There seems to be an assumption that information will emerge naturally on how pupils are progressing towards each of the attainment targets for each of the various outcomes (but not, it appears, on each strand). The directions for reporting to parents emphasize the need also to include more general information about the school's knowledge of the pupil and about appropriate "next steps in learning". Reporting to pupils themselves is given prominence. The importance of feedback to help them become aware of, and contribute consciously to, their own learning is stressed.

During the first round of testing in the Spring of 1991, many parents withdrew their children from testing. This is possible in Scotland as the legal priority is for parents' educational choice. The government at first said that withdrawal was unacceptable and that local authorities would be expected to take legal action against such parents. Several local authorities indicated that they would not do so, and the Minister then said that no action would be taken against the authorities that refused to pursue parents. As a result of the widespread withdrawal, the Minister agreed that in future the tests be used at the discretion of teachers to support their assessment at any point during the relevant year. This, of course, is a very significant change.

The Scottish national assessment system is also different from that for England and Wales in that, as well as not being used as an accountability device for schools, it is not perceived as being able to comment on national standards. It is accepted that a different form of assessment is required for this purpose. Thus, the Assessment of Achievement Programme (AAP), the Scottish version of the English APU, has not been disbanded and will continue to carry out sample surveys to comment on standards of performance.

New forms of assessment

As the first section of this chapter makes clear, pupil assessment in England is replete with new developments: national assessment, GCSE, reform of A and AS level, and the introduction of new general vocational qualifications. Each of these has been described in some detail since this is vital to understanding the current developments in assessment 5-18. This section will be therefore relatively brief. Similarly, the new national curriculum has also been described since it is not possible otherwise to understand the national assessment developments.

These new developments all attempt to embrace new styles of assessment: criterion-referencing, teacher-based assessment, active process-based assessment tasks, and course work assessment. This shift in assessment paradigm from a broadly psychometric, norm-referenced, examination-based model towards an educational assessment model is well illustrated by the philosophy outlined by the TGAT report. Teacher assessment, it said, should be a fundamental element of the system and the information should serve several purposes: formative, diagnostic, summative (to record the overall achievement of a pupil in a systematic way) and evaluative (so that aspects of the work of a school could be assessed). The report was acknowledged as being far-sighted, professionally supportive and likely to encourage good practice in assessment and teaching. There were, however, criticisms from some educationists of the 10-level system, concerns over the extent of external testing, the playing-down of teacher assessment in relation to SATs and the publication of unadjusted national assessment results as a basis for school accountability.

The move towards criterion-referencing, continuous assessment based on teacher judgement and active or extended assessment tasks are common to GCSE and national assessment. The latter two elements are time-consuming for teachers but are seen as contributing to their professional role. Where the teacher-based assessments are to be linked with external assessment and/or reported as part of a certification procedure, external moderation is involved, which is also time and resource-consuming.

Other recent developments in assessment practice in the United Kingdom include graded assessment, Records of Achievement and SCOTVEC modules. Graded assessment developed from attempts to modularise the curriculum and to offer pupils shorter-term goals and individual rates of progression through the curriculum. The assessments themselves can be either classroom-based or examination-based, although the latter is difficult to reconcile with the notion of readiness -- that is, taking the assessment only when ready to pass -- which is a crucial element in the argument for the motivating properties of graded assessment. Graded assessment has been a popular development at secondary school level, in maths and modern languages in particular, and teachers report increased student motivation, notably among the less able. There are, however, organisational problems relating to management and flexibility, and technical problems relating to the hierarchical ordering of material and the grade descriptions on the certificates awarded. Problems of developing statements which express unambiguous hierarchies of attainment, the level of specificity of criteria and the generalisability of performance beyond the context of the assessment are the same as those raised by other forms of criterion-referenced assessment. A number of graded assessment schemes have been made equivalent to GCSE, but since the edict about the amount of terminal examination assessment required for GCSE, their future is in doubt. Graded assessment, then, is built on a model of learning which requires learners to have clear information on learning objectives and regular feedback; thus, it is more interactive than the traditional secondary school examination and course.

The model underlying profiles and Records of Achievement (RoA) is rather more interactive and dynamic. It also involves stating objectives but these should be discussed and negotiated with the pupil. Dialogue with the pupils should include reflections on their attainment, and through dialogue pupils should come to accept more responsibility for their own learning. The content of the RoA is also wider than the narrowly academic: it is an attempt to provide more comprehensive, constructive and meaningful records of pupils' achievement in school, emanating from an era in which public examinations were aimed only at the top 60 per cent of the ability range. "Profiling" is the procedure in which pupils and teachers jointly construct an assessment record over a wide range of academic and personal objectives. The RoA is the summative document which results from the profiling process and which pupils have when they leave school or college. This is sometimes known as descriptive reporting or assessment, and the limitation on it as far as accountability or evaluative procedures are concerned, is that the descriptions are not amenable to numerical or grade-based summarising. Indeed, the proponents of RoA would be against such a move since modifying the summative document to produce quantitative descriptors would jeopardise the nature of the profiling process and the centrality of the formative, teacher-pupil interaction.

RoAs have been essentially a grass-roots development, mostly at secondary level. In 1984 the government said that it was committed to RoAs for all school-leavers by the end of that decade. In 1990 the DES Regulations on reporting pupil achievements were called Records of Achievement, but the requirement is simply for a document of record, not for the profiling process which leads up to it. This process is not forbidden: indeed the Regulations state that what is being legislated for is the minimum and that good practice will suggest more. This good practice is, however, time-consuming and given the range of legally required activities, it is not clear to what extent the full RoA process will survive.

In Scotland a new form of assessment was introduced by the government's Action Plan in 1983 for young people aged 16-18. The curriculum for students not studying full-time for the traditional SCE (Scottish Certificate of Education) Highers exams was reconstructed to be taught in modules, normally of 40 hours' duration, in both general and vocational subjects. The content of each module is carefully defined in "descriptors" which can be conveyed to students at the beginning of the course. The student's work in appropriate assignments is assessed at the end of the module by the tutor, on a pass/fail basis: but students who fail can immediately make a second attempt. Pass work is rewarded by a National Certificate awarded by SCOTVEC (Scottish Vocational Education Council) and modules may be grouped to satisfy requirements for specific vocational qualifications. Over 2.000 modules are now available, though any one institution may offer only a selection of these. It is expected that a full-time student may complete 24 modules in one year.

The modular system offers considerable flexibility in planning a course of studies, and it has been welcomed by students as eliminating the stresses of end-of-year examinations and as giving them evidence of progress at frequent intervals. Modules have been used by pilot schools in the TVEI programme (Technical and Vocational Education Initiative): they are also used not only in colleges of further education but in general secondary schools, allowing students to combine preparation for the customary SCE external exams with study by this other means, gaining a wider curricular approach. Yet some questions about modules have still to be resolved. Although there is a SCOTVEC system of moderation and inspection, a great deal is left to individual tutors' judgement. Students may rely too greatly on the ease with which they can resit and so produce work which barely meets the required standard. Some critics complain that the pass/fail result does not give sufficient information as to whether a student has performed excellently or merely at a passable level. On a longer-term perspective, it is questioned whether students retain the knowledge acquired during the relatively brief period of module study

-- though this question of retention can be raised for traditional forms of assessment too. Nevertheless, the innovation of modular teaching and testing is considered to be of very great value: and the use of modules is now being extended to the Higher National Certificate -- that is, to some parts of higher education.

Issues

The GCSE with its certificating role is a classic example of a "high stakes" assessment, and it is clear that it has had an effect on curriculum and pedagogy. The national assessment SATs for England and Wales are also "high stakes" (since pupils, schools and possibly teachers will be evaluated on the basis of results) and there is preliminary evidence that the style and content of the SATs for 7-year-olds are influencing infant teachers' practice. In both these cases, the moves are towards what educationists would regard in the main as better practice: a move away from restrictive teaching and learning styles and, at seven, towards working with small groups of children. In both cases also, the central role of teachers in the assessment process has contributed to their professional development and engagement.

These trends, however, appear to be in danger of reversal: the government is not in favour of course work assessment, time-consuming SATs, or teacher assessment dominating at certificating or reporting stages. The move is therefore back towards the domination of traditional examination procedures and paper-and-pencil exercises with all that this will mean for classroom practice. That said, the traditional examination procedures are not of the multiple-choice type but allow for assessment of extended essay writing and higher-order thinking skills: thus, they already involve the performance, or authentic, assessments which the United States is seeking.

The feasibility, and effect, of working to a defined progression of teaching and learning, with its underlying concept of linear progression which is at odds with constructivist models of learning, has yet to be judged. The effect of having high-status external assessment in only the core can be predicted, yet the fact that the rest of the curriculum is legislated may soften the effect. It is, however, a significant reversal of the move towards an educational model of assessment, and it is important to ask why this has happened.

Assessment is being used by this administration, as by many others, to gear up the education system, to raise standards and to force accountability on schools. In this climate, teachers are not to be trusted as their own evaluators. Neither are "elaborate, time-consuming" assessment tasks considered appropriate. The formal, unseen examination has served the system well in the past, so the argument goes, and will do so again. It is seen as more objective, reliable and cheaper. It is also felt by many traditionalists that the more open relationship between teacher and pupil, which is a strength of the RoA movement, for example, is inappropriate.

There are two fundamental issues which, in the case of national assessment, have contributed to this reversal of fortune. The first lies in the TGAT model itself. In the TGAT report there was little mention of standards and how these could be raised by testing, and limited emphasis on accountability procedures. The tone of the report was thus at odds with the political climate within which national curriculum and assessment was introduced. Small wonder then that, as teachers complained of the workload involved in SATs and the low level of standardization became clear, the Prime Minister said the "SATs" for 1992 would be largely paper-and-pencil tests, standardized, and capable of being taken by the whole class at once. In addition, the model of assessment (based as it was on teacher assessment and emphasizing formative and diagnostic purposes, summative being kept to 16, with a range of types of task and response mode) is essentially one that is not suited to surveying the performance of every pupil of a particular age group at a certain point in time, particularly given the complex structure of the national curriculum to which it is linked. The national assessment blueprint thus did not support the administration's requirements. Add to that the apparent lowering of standards in GCSE and the administration clearly felt that it was time to call a halt to these particular educational developments.

The second issue is that the model as it was being articulated simply did not work. Given a complex and detailed criterion-referenced assessment system, it may be possible to require teachers to assess every child on every criterion and to report this four times during their school career, but it is not possible to link this with external, project-type assessment of every pupil on a high proportion of the criteria, at a particular point in the school year. It is simply too time-consuming, and if both the TA and the SATs have to be moderated externally in order to provide for comparability, the task becomes even more daunting.

The authors of the TGAT report maintain that their plan has been misinterpreted, hence the problems; but there are, nevertheless, major technical problems inherent in the blueprint (Gipps, 1991). And to suggest that summative assessment could wait until 16 when reporting was required at all four ages was naive, to say the least. What is almost more surprising is why the TGAT report was accepted in the first place, given the political agenda.

The model of assessment articulated by TGAT is one which emphasizes professional, detailed, formative assessment by teachers. Even the SATs' major function in 1991 is likely to have been formative: the detailed, ecologically-valid tasks have been high on teacher feedback and pupil enjoyment, but low on reliability. For information on the performance of schools and classes, different approaches are required. Testing using quicker, more reliable instruments is one way; sample surveying using more complex instruments is another; regular inspections and reports on schools will also provide the community with information about how well schools are doing, particularly at primary level where the introduction of certificating procedures is seen as less appropriate; at secondary level public examination results can be used, preferably in relation to progress scores of students (the "value added" by the school).

The notion that one programme of assessment could fulfil four functions (formative, diagnostic, summative and evaluative) has been shown to be false: different purposes require different models of assessment (and different relationships between teacher and pupil). It may be possible to design one assessment system which measures performance for accountability and selection purposes whilst at the same time supporting the teaching/learning process, but we do not yet have the technology to do so.

There are three lessons to be learnt from recent developments in the United Kingdom: good quality assessment is time-consuming and requires commitment; the two general functions of assessment are difficult to reconcile; assessment frameworks which do not support the aims of a powerful administration are unlikely to survive.

The Scottish experience is particularly pertinent here: the government does not have a strong base in Scotland; teachers are better organised professionally than in England; and parents have stronger educational rights. The result is that the role of external tests has changed from checking on teachers' assessments to supporting them. Add to this the absence of any requirement to publish school results to enable comparison and the Scottish model can be seen as weaker on the accountability side and stronger on the professional side. This is in direct contrast to the direction of developments in the rest of the United Kingdom.

The difference between the educational body and the political body is not just one of ideology, but also of power. It is however the case that enforced change does not always wipe out previous practice. There have been sufficient developments in the United Kingdom involving good practice in assessment, with teachers who have been involved in them convinced of their educational value, that it may be possible for these techniques, approaches and attitudes to survive the return to narrow testing practice with all that this will mean for teaching and learning.

REFERENCES

DEPARTMENT OF EDUCATION AND SCIENCE (DES) (1984), *Records of Achievement: a statement of policy.* London: HMSO.

-- (1987), *The National Curriculum 5-16: A Consultation Document.* DES/Welsh Office.

-- (1988), *National Curriculum: Task Group on Assessment and Testing: A Report.* DES/Welsh Office.

-- (1990a), Circular 8/90 *Records of Achievement* 10/7/90.

-- (1990b), Circular 9/90 *ERA 1988 : The Education (National Curriculum)(Assessment Arrangements for English, Mathematics and Science) Order 1990* 23/7/90.

-- (1991), *Education and Training for the 21st Century* Volume I. London: HMSO.

GIPPS, C. (1990), *Assessment: A teacher's guide to the issues.* London: Hodder & Stoughton.

GIPPS, C. (1991), *National Assessment: a Research Agenda.* London: University of London Institute of Education.

NORTHERN IRELAND SCHOOLS EXAMINATION AND ASSESSMENT COUNCIL (1991), *Pupil Assessment in Northern Ireland: Arrangements at Key Stages 1, 2 and 3.* Advice to Lord Belstead, Jan. 1991, NISEAC, and the response from Lord Belstead to Professor Desmond Rea, Chairman of NISEAC 27.2.91.

PRAIS, S. and WAGNER, K. (1983), *Schooling Standards in Britain and Germany.* London: National Institute for Economic and Social Research.

SCOTTISH EDUCATION DEPARTMENT (1987), *Curriculum and Assessment in Scotland - A Policy for the 90s.* Edinburgh: SED/HMSO,

-- (1990), *The Testing in Primary Schools (Scotland) Regulations 1990.* Edinburgh: SED/HMSO.

Chapter 8

THE UNITED STATES OF AMERICA

by
Professor John Nisbet
University of Aberdeen

For the past 50 years and more, United States has been foremost in the use and development of standardized tests in education. The country pioneered the development of standardized multiple-choice tests in the pre-1940 era; and now, each year, 127 million standardized tests mandated by states and districts are applied, and 20 million school days are devoted to this testing (ETS, 1990a). In the 1970s, in response to concern about national standards, states introduced compulsory testing of "basic skills": by 1982, 39 of the 50 states had "minimum competency" test programmes, and by 1989/90, 47 states required testing at some stage of primary or secondary education. In the 1980s, the emphasis shifted from "minimum competency" to "excellence", and in or around 1983, no fewer than 29 national reports were published on the theme of the need to improve national standards of attainment in education. (The years 1990/91 may match that record.)

Underlying this concern is a belief that United States is falling behind other industrialised countries and that the schools are to blame.

> "Our nation is at risk. Our once unchallenged pre-eminence... is being overtaken by competitors throughout the world." (*A Nation at Risk*, 1983, National Commission on Excellence in Education, p. 5)

> "The nation's schools are in trouble." (*Making the Grade*, 1983, 20th Century Fund, p. 3)

> "The possibility that other nations may outstage us... is suddenly troubling Americans."(*Action for Excellence*, 1983, Educational Commission of the States, p. 13)

> "Our children could be stragglers in a world of technology. We must not let this happen." (*Educating Americans for the 21st Century*, 1983, p.v.

Murphy's (1990) review of this period quotes 58 examples of evidence of "failure of schools" or "need for reform", from reports between 1983 and 1989, and of these two-thirds (38) derive from the results of testing. Thus, testing has fuelled concern over the nation's schools; and more extensive testing, national and statewide, is seen by many as the leverage for raising standards. One of six national goals set by President Bush in 1990 is that:

"By the year 2000... US students will be first in the world in science and mathematics achievement."

The educational programme to achieve these goals, *America 2000*, announced in April 1991, includes national examinations at grades 4, 8 and 12 (approximate ages 10, 14 and 18) in mathematics, science, English, history and geography.

The rationale of these test programmes is that testing, by focusing teaching and learning on what is tested, ensures coverage of basic elements in the curriculum. Publication of results, a key element for "leverage" on standards, applies the pressure of accountability on teachers and administrators as a stimulus to higher standards (though not a guarantee). Bluntly (to quote from one interview), "any superintendent who wants to keep his job will take action to improve his district's test average". Critics challenge both these arguments, questioning the assumptions that poor standards are to be blamed on lack of effort or neglect of basics, or that testing will raise standards.

"National tests would no more solve educational problems than giving every child an X-ray would solve hunger problems among children."
(Schuman, 1991).

A second broad theme in the current scene is the groundswell of reaction against excessive testing, and especially against the limitations of standardized tests. Multiple-choice tests in particular are criticised, not only by teachers and educationists but also by the students themselves and by many of the public, on the grounds that they narrow the curriculum, distort teaching and learning, encourage outmoded drill-and-practice, discourage (or even reject) the hard-to-teach child and diminish the professional role of teachers in the classroom (Shepard, 1991a). Excessive testing has left many students unpractised in handling complex tasks, even in writing consecutive prose and inexperienced in applying their knowledge in problem-solving and critical reasoning.

"Current testing, predominantly multiple choice in format, is over-relied upon... To help promote greater development of the talents of all our people, alternative forms of assessment must be developed and more critically judged and used, so that testing and assessment open gates of opportunity rather than close them off."
(National Commission on Testing and Public Policy, 1990, pp. ix-x)

Criticisms such as these have resulted in proposals to modify the design of standardized tests, towards more open-ended questions and attempts to assess higher-order thinking skills. A strong lobby argues for more than this, to replace (or at least complement) short-answer tests with "alternative assessment", or "authentic assessment", extended tasks of the kind one meets in every-day situations:

"real instances... rather than proxies or estimators... The tasks and problems used in authentic assessments are complex, integrated and challenging instructional tasks. They require children to think... Thus performance assessments mirror good instruction, which engages children in thinking from the very beginning." (Shepard, 1991b)

The term "alternative assessment" is sometimes used in the United States to refer to essay examinations and question forms which would be regarded as standard in other countries (a point which illustrates the dominance of objective testing in the US approach to assessment); but it also includes a range of innovative procedures which are being developed with characteristic American vigour.

These two themes, national standards and alternative forms of assessment, provide the framework for this review of assessment issues in the United States.

National standards

In the absence of any national examination system in the United States, the agency responsible for "The Nation's Report Card" is the National Assessment of Educational Progress (NAEP), located in the Educational Testing Service (ETS) at Princeton. Since its foundation in the 1960s, it has monitored standards with the voluntary co-operation of states, using a matrix sampling design which limits the burden of testing and does not yield test scores for individual students. Publication of state average scores was debarred until June 1991, when these were released for the first time. Testing currently covers 37 states and 130 000 students annually, in grades 4, 8 and 12 in English, mathematics, science, history and civics and geography, together with supplementary data on social background, learning environment and teacher practice.

> "NAEP is not a testing program (and) not a research project, but rather it should be considered as an information system." (Lapointe, 1990)

NAEP is thus uniquely placed to review national standards over 20 years of testing:

> "Students' current achievement levels are far below those that might indicate competency... Overall achievement levels are little different entering the 1990s than they were two decades earlier... In recent assessments, more students appear to be gaining basic skills, yet fewer are demonstrating a grasp of higher-level applications of these skills... Despite progress in narrowing the gaps, the differences in performance between white students and their minority counterparts remain unacceptably large... Across the past 20 years little seems to have changed in how students are taught. Classrooms still appear to be dominated by textbooks, teacher lectures and short-answer activity sheets." (NAEP, 1990, pp. 9-10).

NAEP is sensitive to criticisms of short-answer tests: new methods of testing, incorporating some of the techniques of "alternative assessment", are being incorporated in the surveys planned for 1992 in mathematics, reading and writing. The 1992 reading assessment, for example, will include longer passages, most of the items will be aimed at higher-order thinking, and some 40 per cent of the questions will be open-ended (Cross, 1990; NAEP, 1991).

The Educational Testing Service is also responsible for US participation in international surveys, the International Evaluation of Achievement (IEA) and its own programme, the International Assessment of Educational Progress (IAEP). Results of international surveys have tended to increase public concern, with the United States showing poorly in comparison to countries such as Japan. Warnings against over-simple comparisons, pointing to national differences in social structure, cultural homogeneity, educational expenditure and family support for education, tend to be overlooked by the media in reporting results (Howe, 1991).

The results of other national testing also are sometimes quoted as indicators of standards. The Scholastic Aptitude Test (SAT), for example, is taken by many applicants for college entrance. A progressive decline in average SAT scores has attracted wide public attention, though the changing composition of the test-taking group (increased numbers, greater minority representation, etc.) probably accounts for as much as 50 per cent of the decline (Howe, 1985). The SAT is also currently being modified to include a larger element of extended writing and 20 per cent open-ended items.

Monitoring of standards is also carried out by the states, as education is a state responsibility. Since the 1970s, states have instituted mandatory test programmes, and, as always in the United States, there is wide variety among the states. Almost all the testing takes the form of standardized tests, but states use the results in different ways. For example, Wilson and Corbett (1990) compared the provision in 1986/87 in two states, Maryland and Pennsylvania, representing a contrast between high- and low-stakes testing. (The level of stakes is the extent to which those affected see the tests as "used to make important decisions that immediately and directly affect them"; Madaus, 1988.) Pennsylvania testing was initially low-stakes, with a focus on identifying students in need of additional instruction; while Maryland required students to "pass" multiple-choice tests in four subjects to receive a high school diploma. Subsequent publication of school average scores had the effect of raising the stakes, and districts increasingly gave "single-minded devotion to specific, almost game-like ways to raise test scores".

In state testing, as with NAEP, new styles of testing are being introduced: for example in Boston, California, Connecticut, Maryland and Vermont (to quote a few states recently cited by the US Department of Education; Cross, 1991). The federal contribution to this trend has been to fund research and development work on testing in a number of centres, primarily to the new Center for Research on Evaluation, Standards and Student Testing (CRESST) in Los Angeles, which has a $15 million grant over a five-year period. A recent CRESST report found that over half the states are involved to some degree in new styles of "performance assessment" other than extended writing tasks.

State Governors have set up a Commission with a number of working groups to advise on how to achieve the National Goals set out in America 2000. Meetings of this "Goals Panel" have attracted wide interest and sessions have even been relayed on television. An interim report (Resnick, 1991) offered recommendations for the 1991 national assessment and for an end-of-decade national assessment system. The 1991 "Nation's Report Card" should be based on NAEP surveys (the "best currently available data"), ETS Advanced Placement tests, high school course enrolments, international comparisons and an opinion poll of clients, but not SAT or other selectively taken tests. The end-of-decade proposals envisage a national examining system on a decentralised "cluster" model, calibrated through "national anchor examinations" which "must be focussed on high levels of achievement (thinking, reasoning, etc., not routinized skills), tied to curriculum goals or frameworks, and designed to be studied for and taught to".

Murphy (1990), reviewing the recent history of educational reform in the United States, identified three "waves". The first wave, lasting to 1985, was characterised by the concept of "repair", through minimum competency testing and an extension of state control. The second wave, 1986-89, shifted to the concept of "restructure", based on a drive for professional staff development among teachers as well as empowering parents, using test results to identify and emphasize priorities for reform. The third wave, he suggests, is one of "redesign", based on new and deeper insights into teaching and learning. Since this was written, however, the initiative of the President and Governors in the *America 2000* programme seems to have reinstated the older model, with its emphasis on centrally-designed national testing and publication of results to ensure greater accountability of schools and teachers.

National testing is not without its critics and sceptics, some hostile to the whole idea, others critical of the way it is done, but the majority unhappy about the way it is (or might be) used. Critics question whether one can raise standards merely by testing, complain of waste of money and teaching time since the results tell teachers nothing new, or see national testing as federal interference in a state responsibility.

Public opinion polls indicate that three-quarters of the public favour national testing, though many parents think that their own children are receiving a satisfactory education and give high grades to public schools in their own communities (a finding interpreted by NAEP, 1990, as evidence of "a false sense of security"). A common public attitude is to ask: what have schools to hide if they object to open examination of their weaknesses?

Among those critical of how testing is done, FairTest in Massachusetts, the National Center for Fair and Open Testing, is an agency which promotes public discussion on educational testing. FairTest wants to see the quantity of testing in schools reduced, argues that results from norm-referenced standardized tests should not be used for critical decisions about individual students, and recommends a move from multiple-choice testing to performance-based assessments.

The main concern is about the use of the results, particularly when these are published in the form of league tables of districts or individual schools, if no account is taken of differences in catchment areas and social background. Publication raises the level of "stakes" and applies pressure on teachers and administrators to concentrate on what is tested and to produce higher test scores, whether or not these represent actual higher achievement. Testing is seen as a crude, indirect and possibly invalid method of institutional management which "deskills" professional judgement: if its effect is to change teachers' and students' behaviour, it is liable to do so in undesirable ways.

Many schools, even progressive private schools, continue to apply standardized tests annually, often towards the end of session. One reason is that, in the absence of any national or state examination, the grades allotted by teachers may assume great importance to parents and employers. Grades based solely on the teachers' own judgement are open to challenge, and comparability between schools is uncertain. As protection against accusations of bias (and even possible legal action), scores on standardized tests are helpful and carry more conviction than unsupported teachers' grades.

Alternative forms of assessment

"Alternative assessment" is variously referred to as "authentic assessment", "performance testing" or "instructional assessment". The prime aim of this approach is to design methods of assessment which will influence teaching and learning positively in ways which contribute to realising educational objectives, requiring realistic (or "authentic") tasks to be performed and focusing on relevant content and skills (such as extended writing or problem-solving). There is a strong groundswell of support -- for example, the 1990 Annual Report of the Educational Testing Service states:

> "There is a need for new kinds of assessments that represent desired educational goals and contribute in constructive ways to the teaching and learning process. Many see the use of well-designed performance tasks in tests (along with, or instead of, multiple-choice questions) as bringing us closer to these aims. We share that view." (ETS, 1990b)

In this approach, the distinction between assessment and instruction is blurred: assessment is not an artificially separate event but an integral part of instruction. In formative assessment it guides the interaction of teacher and student; in summative assessment it identifies objectives for teaching and learning. When assessment tasks are thus brought into line with instructional content and aims, then teaching to the test is legitimate and studying for the examination becomes constructive and worthwhile. This, it is claimed, is the genuine way to raise standards. Mandatory testing aims to raise standards indirectly through the pressure of accountability, but any rise in average test score may reflect only a spurious improvement in test-taking skills. Authentic assessment aims to raise standards directly by improving teaching and learning, relating testing closely to instruction so that its influence on the classroom will (hopefully) be beneficial.

A recent ETS newsletter (1990a) refers to

> "some consensus within what might be called 'the educational testing reform movement' as to the general directions testing needs to go if educational objectives are to be achieved."

These changes of direction may take the form of modifications to the conventional style of standardized testing, or they may be radical departures from that style. The limitations of multiple-choice testing, noted earlier in this review and widely acknowledged, have led to modifications in the type of questions asked in tests. There is wider use of open-ended questions which require a constructed response. To allow machine scoring, ingenious procedures have been introduced: for example, a 10 x 10 grid for numerical answers which provides 100 options, and "figural responses" in which students draw arrows to indicate direction, make marks to indicate location, interpret data and sketch graphs, scanned, analysed and scored by computers. More complex tasks are set, to avoid the fragmentation of short-answer tests: students are asked to write brief essays to demonstrate their ability to solve problems, interpret data, draw conclusions and organise logical arguments; and reading tests use longer passages or even books from the students' course work. Test questions are designed which require students to think independently and which "model sustained thoughtfulness" (Wolf et al. 1990) rather than routine responses.

Alternative assessment, however, usually implies a more radical departure from conventional testing. Dwyer (1990) writes of "a fundamental paradigm shift from an emphasis on prediction and control to an emphasis on meaning and understanding"; and Wolf et al. (1990) state:

> "The design and implementation of these new forms of assessments will entail nothing less than a wholesale transition from what we call a 'testing culture' to an 'assessment culture'."

The terms, authentic assessment, performance testing and instructional assessment, have been defined earlier in this chapter: they are used to describe "instructionally relevant methods of assessment" and "a conceptual approach to assessment which brings together instructional theory and assessment methodology" (quotations from interviews), in that the test material is essentially similar to the tasks involved in the regular learning processes in the classroom. Continuous assessment of course work is one form of this approach; and there is extensive experimentation with "portfolios" or records of achievement.

Portfolios are familiar in the arts as collections of a student's best work. In this context, in a wider meaning of the term, a portfolio is a record of a student's learning in any subject (usually with the student's reflections on the work presented), which is then assessed as a full-scale presentation of work covered and the student's strengths and weaknesses. In Harvard, Project Zero and Arts Propel are exploring the development of this form of assessment -- which they prefer to call "a process-folio", since the folios are regarded as "instruments of learning rather than showpieces of final accomplishment" (Gardner, 1990). The students' reflections on their work, the reasons for their choice of work presented, the inclusion of early drafts and especially their self-evaluations, all are important elements in a learning process in which assessment is primarily feedback to the student who is given valuable experience in self-monitoring. Clearly, for those accustomed to thinking of assessment in conventional ways, scoring presents problems (see below). ETS, Research for Better Schools (Philadelphia), California, Connecticut, New York, Pittsburgh and Vermont are among many experimenting with this form of assessment. ETS introduced Writing Portfolios in its 1990 national assessment programme, "to measure the quality of student writing produced outside the assessment situation" (ETS, 1990c). Teachers of grades 4 and 8 were given broad guidelines to use in selecting pieces of writing for submission -- particularly "process writing" (gathering information, drafting, editing, etc) requiring important skills and strategies which cannot be assessed by conventional testing.

A 1991 FairTest pamphlet lists the growing number of states which have begun to implement alternative or authentic assessment procedures - North Carolina, California, Mississippi, Connecticut, Arizona, Vermont, Georgia, New

York and Missouri -- and reports that 28 states now use essays instead of multiple-choice tests to evaluate writing.

Alternative assessment is not easy to implement. It makes a greater demand, not less, than conventional examining, and it raises a number of problems: scoring, subjectivity, validity and reliability; comparability between schools, between teachers and between students; and cost. The last of these is discussed in the "Issues" section which follows; procedures seeking to cope with the other problems are briefly reviewed below.

The production of a score is not seen by the advocates of alternative assessment as its main function. Essentially, alternative assessment is not another route to providing the information now offered by normative tests: it implies a fundamental change of attitude to assessment redefining its function in education. Nevertheless, criticisms of its subjectivity, difficulties of marking and the need for checks for fairness and comparability are recognised as important issues to be faced. The *New York Times* (24 April, 1991), for example, expressed "the worry that a portfolio could place children at the mercy of impressionistic evaluation".

Scoring, when it is seen as appropriate, is usually criterion-referenced and not norm-referenced, or takes the form of an overall impression mark. A more complex form of recording and reporting performance is the use of "profiles", presenting a pattern of scores on different aspects. This avoids the problem of "aggregation": the questionable validity of combining "chalk and cheese" -- for example, adding marks for accuracy and marks for creativity to produce a spurious "average" score. In the use of portfolios, there is still a wide variety of practice, on what and how much should be included, the best samples or a record to demonstrate progress, who makes the selection of items for inclusion, and what criteria should be used in assessment. Conventional testing is judged in terms of validity and reliability, but these terms require redefinition if they are to be applied to alternative assessment. For example, Fredericksen and Collins (1989) suggest the term, "systemic validity", to describe

> "the effects of instructional changes brought about by the introduction of a test into an educational system. A systemically valid test is one that induces... curricular and instructional changes that foster the development of the cognitive skills that the test is designed to measure."

-- or, we might add, foster development of the knowledge and skills specified in the curricular objectives. Messick (1989) suggests the concept of "consequential validity" to refer to the impact of a test on classroom teaching.

To establish standards for comparability (and thus for possible use in accountability), "collaborative assessment" -- monitoring by other teachers in panels -- is widely used, though this adds substantially to the labour and cost involved. An alternative approach is the use of a reference scale of samples of student performance to assist teachers in their assessments. A good example of this comes not from the United States but across the border, in the Toronto Benchmarks Program:

"Benchmarks are samples of student performances on a wide range of language and mathematics tasks... in grades 3, 6 and 8... typical examples of what students in these grades can read; how well they write; how well they compute, measure and apply mathematics to everyday problems; and how well they speak and enter into discussion... Five different levels of performance are identified with the examples given." (Benchmarks Fact Sheet 6, May 1991).

Also from the same region, the Ontario Assessment Instruments Pool distinguishes initial assessment, formative assessment and summative evaluation, and for each of these functions offers a range of techniques -- tests, interviews, self-assessment instruments, targets, checklists and observation (with guidelines on criteria and indicators to note) -- as well as curriculum resource units to be used to assist in assessment.

Thus, alternative assessment need not imply a radical abandonment of the conventional uses of assessment. However, many of the supporters of alternative assessment question whether it is reconcilable with the use of tests for accountability purposes. This is the first of three issues reviewed in the concluding section.

Issues

1. *The conflicting requirements of public accountability and instructional improvement*

The latest ETS Annual Report (1990b) carries an extensive discussion of this issue. Accountability testing is a response to the public demand for evidence of the educational impact of the "billions of tax dollars invested annually in schools". But from teachers, school administrators and parents, there is a demand for "assessments that can guide the improvement of teaching and learning".

"Ideally, such assessment should itself be a vehicle for individual learning, rather than an impersonal snapshot of a national or regional sample. It has been difficult for these two purposes -- public accountability and instructional improvement -- to be served by the same kind of test."

Accountability testing does not fit easily with instruction: it is an imposed system, usually relying on multiple-choice machine-scored tests to hold down costs, and too often used to make superficial judgements. New performance measures do not fit with accountability: they are closely tied to work done in individual classrooms and with individual students, are more expensive to operate, and do not readily yield simple scores which can be used normatively to assess trends in standards.

"ETS is involved in an intensive development effort that may help to reduce the gap between instructional assessment and accountability assessment, and may improve both in the process. For accountability purposes, we are developing performance measures that would be relatively inexpensive to administer on a large scale. For instructional assessment, there are research and development projects now under way to construct instruments that will both evaluate and facilitate student learning."

This attractive compromise, using both conventional and alternative forms to complement each other, has the obvious drawback that the two forms are based on conflicting philosophies and serve very different functions, and in "high stakes" conditions the conventional is likely to dominate classroom practice. Problems of comparability in the new forms of assessment and doubts about teachers' subjective judgements load the balance in favour of the *status quo*.

The idea of designing a single form of assessment which will perform a variety of functions with equal success is seen by most writers on assessment as a mistaken objective, preferring the use of different forms for different functions. Teachers are accustomed to using different forms of assessment for summative, formative and diagnostic purposes; and most would probably accept that accountability requires a different style from the day-to-day assessment within the classroom -- asking only that accountability testing be kept from taking too prominent a part.

The issue here is not just what form assessment should take, but what uses are made of it, and how these uses are perceived by students, parents and teachers. If crucial decisions on individuals are to be made on the results, or if scores are published in a competitive league table, teachers can turn any form of assessment into drill -- even "authentic assessment" (for example by coaching in model answers, or, in writing, by training in standard patterns or stock phrases). In a "low stakes" context, by contrast, the prospects for effective use of a variety of methods for a variety of purposes seem more hopeful.

2. *Cost*

It would be nice if questions of cost would just go away and leave us free to make decisions solely on the basis of what is best. Obviously, cost should never be the main or sole criterion, but, with inevitably limited resources, increased expenditure or time spent on one aspect means less available for others; and therefore cost is a consideration in determining priorities and choice. Cost includes teachers' time and effort, administrative handling and development work, as well as financial outlay on materials.

Multiple-choice tests are relatively cheap and easy to handle; they can be machine-scored so that large numbers (well over 100 million annually in the United States) can be tested economically; they produce numerical scores on standard scales which can be processed and analysed mechanically. Alternative assessment is time-consuming -- five times as costly as tests, according to one estimate in interview -- and some forms (essay answers, for example) cover a more limited area of the curriculum than a standardized test. ETS reports that one state which redesigned its test programme around performance tasks faced a ten-fold increase in expenditure. A critic (in interview) described alternative assessment as "inefficient... attractive but expensive", especially in teachers' time. "How much information per dollar?" he asked. It is no saving to use a cheap procedure which gives poor results or has a harmful effect; but ideal solutions may be too expensive to consider. One of those interviewed served on a working party in music, which, for lack of funds, was obliged to abandon plans for performance assessment in favour of a paper-and-pencil test!

A hidden cost in some forms of alternative assessment is teachers' time. Whereas in most European countries teachers accept setting and marking their own exercises and examinations (and sometimes discussing work returned to students) as a normal part of their duties, American reliance on multiple-choice tests has created a situation in which teachers may not be ready to accept the extra workload, and time for this work has not been built into their regular programme.

Consequently, the development of alternative assessment must take account of efficiency of operation as well as questions of validity and the effects on classroom practice. A more general issue is what proportion of educational expenditure should be allocated to assessment: perhaps the balance between teaching and testing is already wrong, and a solution which increases outlay on assessment is a move in the wrong direction. However, if assessment can be genuinely integrated with learning, then argument in terms of "how much information per dollar" is misleading.

3. *A new view of assessment?*

Changes in the approach to testing in the United States which have been discussed in this review represent a fundamental paradigm shift which is gaining acceptance but cannot yet be described as a Kuhnian revolution. The emphasis on national testing and standards reflects a firm adherence to older, well-established models of measurement, ability, performance and instruction. The alternative assessment movement links with a constructivist theory of learning, seeing assessment as "part of learning rather than a judgment passed on performance once the learning is over" (Hargreaves, 1989). The ETS Annual Report (1990b) speaks of "a new generation of testing" and describes the task facing ETS as "nothing less than to transform the role of testing in American education".

Wolf *et al.* (1990) set their review of developments in assessment in the context of new theories of learning:

"Any discussion of changing views of student assessment has to be situated in the larger framework of views on learning and education."

Most teaching leaves students in a passive position: we need assessments which stimulate active critical thinking. Constructivist learning theory emphasizes meaning, understanding and structure which have to be created by learners. Learners achieve understanding by active interaction with the content of knowledge, with the teacher, with peers, with experience and with their own reflections on their experiences. Assessment, particularly self-assessment, is an integral part of the process of learning, providing feedback and reinforcement. In recent years, cognitive psychology has increasingly come to recognise the importance of affective and social elements in learning -- attitudes, motivation, relationships and self-image. Learners' perceptions are all-important: their perceptions of the task, of the process and of their own competence. Assessment plays a crucial role in influencing these perceptions. Therefore, one of the criteria for judging an assessment system is its impact on the climate of learning within the educational provision.

A related issue is the role of the teacher in assessment, whether that is to be one of working to prescriptions imposed by external authority or the more professional role of working responsibly to one's own standards and judgement (or, more realistically, how to achieve a balance between these two extremes). Wolf (in interview) suggested an analogy with quality control in industry, which can operate in either of two contrasting ways: by imposing a supervisory layer of inspection, or by building quality control into the process, involving the operatives themselves directly in the maintenance of the highest standards. This latter course demands an educated workforce; and one argument against the more extreme versions of accountability testing is that it excludes the teachers from judgement, and fails to use their skills -- thus, testing deskills the teacher.

Stake (1991) develops this idea by calling attention to teachers' "intuitive, working conceptualization of education" which, he argues, is a prime determinant of what happens in classrooms.

> "Teachers intuitively and ceaselessly assess the progress of students... When teachers assiduously pursue state and district goals, they risk departure from the logic and complexity of their subject matters and departure from the personal nature of education... Increasing the orientation of instruction to uniform standards and test information causes teachers to draw back from their conceptualizations of subject matter to be taught."

If assessment is to be used effectively to raise standards, it must build on, rather than demolish, the teachers' conceptualisation of their task. Higher standards are more likely to be achieved by professional development than by attempts to bypass the teachers' responsibility.

Any substantial change in assessment systems depends on changing public attitudes and assumptions about assessment. Each country has its own "assessment culture", a body of practices established over time and linked with deeply-held values, which (like other cultures) provide a necessary continuity and stability but are strongly resistant to change. Public debate about assessment, though usually seen as unwelcome pressure, has to be seen as an opportunity to create awareness and raise the level of public understanding.

Hargreaves (1989) brings these points together by linking curriculum development, professional development and assessment development:

> "More pupil-based assessment and recording procedures will lead to curriculum development which is more effectively geared to the needs of the individual pupil... Teachers will change themselves as they begin to perceive, through their pupils, a need for change in their practice... In this way, these new patterns of pupil-based assessment develop the pupil, they develop the teacher and they develop the curriculum. Assessment development, pupil development and curriculum development are therefore deeply and inextricably intertwined... There is a desperate need for a coherent, alternative educational strategy

which will tie together curriculum, assessment, teacher and pupil development in a persuasive reform programme which can promise and deliver greater educational equality and opportunity."

REFERENCES

America 2000: An education strategy (1991), Washington DC: US Department of Education.

CROSS, C. T. (1990), "National goals: Four priorities for educational research", *Educational Researcher,* November, pp. 21-23.

CROSS, C. T. (1991), Quoted in *Los Angeles Times,* March 9.

DWYER, C. A. (1990), "Trends in the assessment of teaching and learning: Educational and methodological perspectives", in Broadfoot, P., Murphy, R. and Torrance, H. (eds.), *Changing Educational Assessment: International perspectives and trends,* London: Routledge.

ETS, Educational Testing Service (1990a), *Policy Notes,* volume 2, number 3. Princeton: ETS.

ETS, Educational Testing Service (1990b), *Helping America Raise Educational Standards for the 21st Century: 1990 Annual Report.* Princeton: ETS.

ETS, Educational Testing Service (1990c) *Which assessment contains all these innovations?* Princeton: ETS.

FREDERICKSEN, J. R. and COLLINS, A. (1989), "A systems approach to educational testing", *Educational Researcher,* 19 (9), December, pp. 27-32.

GARDNER, H. (1990), "Assessment in context: The alternative to standardized testing", in Gifford, B. R. and O'Connor, M. C. (eds.), *Future Assessments: Changing Views of aptitude, achievement and instruction,* Boston: Kluwer.

HARGREAVES, A. (1989), *Curriculum and Assessment Reform,* Milton Keynes: Open University Press.

HOWE, H. (1985), "Let's have another SAT decline", *Phi Delta Kappa,* May, pp. 599-602.

HOWE, H. (1991), Harvard Working Conference on Assessment, 1991.

LAPOINTE, A. E. (1990), "NAEP: A National Report Card for education and the public", *The Assessment of National Goals,* Princeton: ETS, pp. 47-62.

MADAUS, G. F. (1988), "The influence of testing on the curriculum", in Tanner, L. (ed.), *Critical Issues in the Curriculum, 87th Yearbook of the NSSE.* Chicago: University of Chicago Press.

MESSICK, S. (1989), "Validity", in Linn, R. L. (ed.) *Educational Measurement* (3rd edition), pp. 13-103.

MURPHY, J. (ed.) (1990), *The Educational Reform Movement of the 1980s*, Berkeley CA: McCutchan.

NAEP, National Assessment of Educational Progress (1990), *America's Challenge: Accelerating academic achievement. A summary of findings from 20 years of NAEP*. Princeton: ETS.

NAEP, National Assessment of Educational Progress (1991), *The Nation's Report Card: Over 20 years on the cutting edge of measurement*, Princeton: ETS.

NATIONAL COMMISSION ON TESTING AND PUBLIC POLICY (1990), *From Gatekeeper to Gateway: Transforming testing in America*, Boston: NCTPP.

SCHUMAN, C. H. (1991), Quoted in *Times Educational Supplement*, April 19.

SHEPARD, L. A. (1991a), "Will national tests improve student learning?", AERA Conference, Washington DC, June 5.

SHEPARD, L. A. (1991b), "Interview on assessment issues", *Educational Leadership*, 20 (2), pp. 21-23 and 27, March.

STAKE, R. E. (1991), "The teacher, standardized tests and prospects of revolution". AERA Conference, Washington DC, June 5.

WILSON, B. L. and CORBETT, H. D. (1990), "Statewide testing and local improvement: An oxymoron?", in Murphy, *op. cit.*, pp. 243-263.

WOLF, D., BIXBY, J., GLEEN, J. III and GARDNER, H. (1990), "To use their minds well: Investigating new forms of student assessment", *Review of Research in Education*, 17, pp. 31-74.

Chapter 9

ISSUES

by
Professor John Nisbet
University of Aberdeen

The country reports in Chapters 2 to 8 show a great diversity of assessment systems, but the systems perform similar functions and raise common recurring issues. In a review of secondary school-leaving examinations in eight countries, Eckstein and Noah (1989a) classify differences among these examinations under seven headings:

- control of the system (government, examination board, school, private);
- uniformity/differentiation (one examination for all, or choice);
- format (method and content);
- control of numbers (selection, allocation);
- retrospective (certification) or prospective (prediction);
- other latent functions (monitoring and motivating); and
- status-conferring (social or vocational importance, as perceived).

In a parallel paper (Eckstein and Noah, 1989b), they conclude that the examination system in a country represents a set of provisional compromises or "trade-offs" among competing values:

"The characteristics of examination systems can serve as indicators of the educational values a nation seeks to uphold. Beyond that, they can serve as pointers to wider political and social values."

Each country has its own priorities and emphases among these values; and so it is unlikely that we can prescribe any one ideal system. Such an ambition is not just unattainable but is probably inappropriate. (This is one of the problems in European Community moves towards "harmonization" of national qualifications among its member states.)

Kellaghan and Madaus (1991) have published a wide-ranging international review of national testing programmes, comparing proposals for the United States with practice in twelve European countries, and identifying issues which will have to be addressed before the form of American national testing can be decided. Combining points from these two reviews with issues sketched in Chapter 1, we can identify a large number of practical issues in the design of assessment systems.

Format

Which methods are to be used for testing and recording achievement: essay-type, multiple-choice, course work; formal or continuous assessment; oral, written or performance measures? What kind of questions should be set: to test knowledge or higher-order reasoning and problem-solving skills? To what extent should teachers' assessments be used, and how are they best combined with externally standardized measures? Which subject areas should be covered, especially in national testing; a basic "core" or all subjects, and how are the creative arts, physical education, health education, religious education, etc., to be assessed? At what level of difficulty should the examinations be set? Should all pupils take the same examination, or should there be differentiation by ability or options within a framework or (in leaving examinations) free choice? Should national testing be by sampling or universal coverage? At which ages or stages should important assessments be made? And which examinations should be compulsory and which optional?

Control

Who will decide these issues? Who will be responsible for constructing, administering and scoring the tests or examinations, oversee security, ensure comparability from year to year and between subjects, and respond to appeals? Will results be made public, for individual pupils, schools, districts, or remain confidential to pupils and parents? Who is the final arbiter on these matters?

Purpose

Is the assessment system primarily formative and diagnostic, to guide and motivate, or is it to be used for selection, prediction and certification, or must it perform both sets of functions simultaneously? Does the purpose change as children grow older? Can assessment provide valid evidence for monitoring and evaluating schools and teachers, districts and even state systems - and how can this best be done so as to assist and not distort the prime aim of promoting learning?

Administrators tend to look to research to provide evidence on which to base decisions on practical issues such as these. The decisions which they seek are within the framework of existing national policies and values, as is appropriate. An international review, however, reveals how different these national policies are. Though it cannot provide straightforward recommendations as solutions to dilemmas, it can contribute to policy-making by highlighting the underlying issues, clarifying options and making values explicit.

The central issue in this review is whether assessment can be used as a means of reforming the curriculum. The converse is certainly true: that assessment, if it remains unchanged, can be an obstacle to reform. By what strategies can changes in assessment help to bring about changes in curriculum?

Our two themes represent two different strategies. National testing can be used as a means of influencing teaching and learning, imposing a national curriculum, applying the pressure of accountability by publishing results in the form of "league tables", and shaping requirements by the content and style of questions asked in the obligatory tests. This is assessment-led curriculum: it is an old strategy, implemented in Great Britain in the 19th century in "Payment by Results", and clearly it is a powerful strategy. It is based on a centre-periphery model of change. National testing need not be used in this way: it can be used merely as a source of information for general monitoring (as in Spain), or diagnostically (as in the testing in France at the start of session).

The other strategy, outlined in many of the new approaches to assessment, shifts the locus of control to teachers and schools, through an assessment system which is more closely integrated with teaching and learning. The use of portfolios or records of achievement, for example, is largely under the control of teachers - and, to some extent, also of the pupils themselves - though there is a strong central element through the provision of guidelines and regulations as to their form and availability. This is a user-centred model, generally adopted in "low stakes" contexts. Of course, the division between the two strategies is not as clear-cut: alternative approaches to assessment can be incorporated in a centre-periphery model, as for example in modifying "minimum competency" tests to assess higher-order abilities.

Setting aside for the moment the link with our two themes, the two strategies for change are best described (to adapt a classification from Bennis et al., 1966) as "coercive" and "re-educative". The coercive method changes teachers' behaviour: the re-educative seeks to change teachers' beliefs, assumptions and values. The weakness of the coercive strategy is that changing behaviour has only superficial effects if beliefs remain unchanged. The weakness of the re-educative strategy is that it is slow, and often unpredictable. In the long term, changing beliefs is the more powerful strategy, though undoubtedly more difficult. It is for this reason that the "alternative assessment" movement, with its focus on the "instructional" use of assessment, represents a potentially more effective line of development for the reform of curriculum. The point is well summarised in the Australian Karmel Report (Australian Schools Commission, 1973):

> "The effectiveness of innovation, no matter at what level it is initiated in a school organisation, is dependent on the extent to which the people concerned perceive a problem and hence realise the existence of a need, are knowledgable about a range of alternative solutions, and feel themselves to be in a congenial organisational climate."

National testing

On the first of the two main themes of this review, it is clear that national testing is here to stay, for the foreseeable future. Its form, however, is still evolving, and will depend on what use is envisaged for it, what purpose it is expected to fulfil, rather than on technical problems of implementation.

Gathering national statistics as an information base for policy is standard procedure in other fields of public expenditure, in employment, balance of payments, housing, agriculture, and so on. At this level, national testing is a monitoring device only (as, for example, in Spain, Chapter 5). It can provide reassurance on standards where there is concern about the many changes in education and in examination procedures: for example, do new teaching methods fail to make adequate demands on children, or does the impressive growth in numbers taking school-leaving examinations reflect a genuine improvement, when the examinations have been changed to meet the needs of this wider population and to incorporate a larger element of course work assessment?

But the purpose of national testing usually goes beyond this. A prime aim claimed for it is that it will raise standards. There are various ways in which it might do this.

At a general level, national testing focuses attention on standards, arousing the attention of the public and of teachers and education administrators. An early example of this is the testing of reading standards in England and Wales by four-yearly national sample surveys from 1948 to 1970. The 1948 survey indicated a serious decline in standards from pre-war levels, but each subsequent survey up to 1970 showed a steady improvement. (Subsequent surveys have shown no significant improvement.) Of course, there is no way of proving any causal effect on testing on standards; but making the results public accentuates the accountability of teachers and schools, providing information for parents and administrators which strengthens their influence. Knowledge about standards should also influence teachers' practice:

> "Teachers receiving information about other schools' practices in teaching and noting the contents of test items are very likely to adapt their own teaching accordingly." (Chapter 4: The Netherlands)

This kind of testing is norm-referenced, but test results can be used to provide diagnostic information about the standards attained by individual pupils (as in France, for example), though in Great Britain teachers complain that the national tests tell them nothing that they do not know already. The use of tests in this way is not possible with sampling, but only if all pupils are tested, a procedure which is enormously costly in money and time.

There is another way in which national testing may affect what is taught in schools, though its influence on standards is debatable. National testing provides a means of control over the curriculum in schools, ensuring that the curriculum truly reflects the agreed priorities, requiring adequate coverage of the knowledge and skills which are considered of prime importance. In some countries, the United Kingdom, Sweden and possibly the United States, national testing is seen as a means to promote a national curriculum. This function is primarily a matter of administrative regulation, though, if appropriately designed tests were set, it could provide a means of influencing the method and content of teaching and learning - for example by requiring problem-solving and the application of knowledge rather than concentrating on factual knowledge only. As we have noted above, the use of assessment as a means of reforming the curriculum is a central theme of this review; but national testing is a relatively crude instrument for achieving reform of this kind. All that can reasonably be asked is that its effect should not be to obstruct reforms which must be achieved by more direct means.

Within these varied aims there is a mixture of formative and coercive strategies. Where national testing goes beyond simply a monitoring exercise, it has usually been presented and implemented as a coercive strategy, with a focus on accountability. This coercive element appears most strongly in the United Kingdom and the United States, where it is criticised as extending the authority of central control and diminishing the autonomy of the teaching profession and the role of local units of administration. The justification offered is that accountability must be enforced: this important function of testing is too important to be entrusted to a professional body, which may be self-protective or reactionary, and therefore it must involve parents (through access to norm-referenced information about their children) and wider democratic control (through publication of results, even as "league tables" of school performance). Germany is the exception: here, there is no national testing, but instead a reliance on the professional judgement of teachers at all levels of the education system. However, as noted in Chapter 3, there is a high degree of teacher accountability of a general kind to education authorities, to pupils and to parents.

National testing has high profile currently in the United Kingdom and the United States, and to a lesser extent in France and the Netherlands. In Sweden, it is a long-established component of the education system. It is used in Spain in a minor role, and not at all in Germany. These differences reflect different traditional attitudes towards educational assessment - "assessment cultures", as they are called in Chapter 1. The concept of "assessment culture" may be used to describe the distinctive pattern of assessment procedures and structures in each country, and the attitudes and values linked with these practices, established over time, providing a necessary continuity and stability but strongly resistant to change. The attempt to specify these "cultures" in detail runs the risk of superficial stereotyping; but we may note, for example, the loyalty to the *Baccalauréat* in France and the *Abitur* in Germany, the commitment to standardized tests in the United States, and the varying emphases between centralised control and local delegation in all the countries reviewed. The term "culture" is justified because the various elements - practices, attitudes, expectations - are interdependent: in Germany, for example, where teachers have relatively high status, assessment procedures rely more on internal school marks (and can include oral testing) than in the United States, where states use standardized tests to an extent which would be unacceptable in Germany. Scandinavian countries are noted for their antipathy to differentiating among people. In France,

> "The long-standing ideological commitment to national unity and equality which has shaped French educational attitudes in the past still produces powerful resistance to any attempt to alter anything which might diminish that unity." (Chapter 2)

In some countries (for example the United States), assessment is part of the public agenda for debate; in Spain, by contrast, Chapter 5 notes the lack of a tradition of public interest and discussion which has inhibited public involvement in reforms. Attempts to change assessment practices must take account of these culturally based public perceptions of the nature and functions of assessment. Inevitably, it seems, change must be slow: can it be accelerated, democratically or top-down, and will national testing assist this process?

New approaches

If national testing is a blunt instrument for higher standards or curriculum reform, requiring coercion to make its impact, then the use of new methods or styles of assessment appears as a more sensitive device for bringing about change. The distinction, of course, is not so clear. For example, new methods of assessment may be introduced into national testing, thus strengthening their influence on the curriculum: this is the strategy proposed in the United States by the Educational Testing Service, and it was a feature of initial plans for national testing in the United Kingdom where, however, the suggested procedures at age 7 (individual reading from books, problem-solving with real materials, etc.: see Chapter 7) proved so demanding of teachers' time - several weeks to test a class - that there is a move to revert to conventional paper-and-pencil tests. However, a distinction can be drawn: whereas national testing necessarily looks towards standardization and applies across schools irrespective of individual differences, the new approaches to assessment outlined in the previous chapters aim to influence individual learners directly, and are more "user-friendly" in the sense that they are designed to fit in with and help promote the individual pupil's learning. Ideally, one would hope to make use of both modes of assessment, for both functions are of value. But they are difficult to reconcile: national testing and national examinations lead towards a "test-driven" curriculum, whereas the new approaches claim to be "curriculum-led".

It is an over-simplification to refer to "new approaches" as if they were all of a type. What are these so-called new approaches? They cover a wide variety: continuous assessment, greater use of course work, extended writing and substantial projects, portfolios or records of achievement, criterion-referenced measures (instead of norm-referenced), "authentic" testing (using materials or contexts similar to those in which the knowledge and skills will be applied, instead of "artificial" paper-and-pencil tests), emphasis in tests and examination questions on problem-solving and knowledge application rather than on recall, and greater reliance on teachers' assessments and on pupils' self-assessment. Using methods such as these, it is claimed, assessment will be more valid and less stressful, and, most important, will support learning more effectively.

Of course, what is new in one country may be already established practice in another: many teachers would reject the description "new" for these methods. Moreover, the introduction of new methods is only a superficial change if the results of assessments continue to be used for the "old" purposes. The common element which justifies use of the term "alternative assessment" to cover this variety of approaches is their shared assumptions about the place and purpose of assessment in learning. This was described in Chapter 1 as viewing assessment "as part of learning, rather than a judgement passed on performance once learning is over" (Hargreaves, 1989). The aim, in this view of assessment, is not to award grades or distinguish the relative merits of individuals, but primarily to encourage learning and influence teaching and learning positively in ways which contribute to realising agreed educational objectives.

The consensus within the "educational reform movement", noted by ETS (1990, see Chapter 8), has been expressed as a resolve to "integrate assessment with teaching and learning". What precisely does this mean? Again, the phrase may cover a variety of aims: that assessment should run in parallel with learning and not as a separate activity; that assessment should be based on the judgements of those who do the teaching and of the learners themselves in self-assessment; and that the design of assessment should fall in line with the objectives determined for the curriculum, and not vice versa.

The underlying principles of this approach derive from a constructivist theory of learning (though not all its advocates would accept this interpretation). Briefly, constructivist theory rests on the premise that learners create their own knowledge, structuring it in their own personal way, in a search for meaning and understanding. Thus, learning involves a personal construction of knowledge.

"Learning is not something that happens to students: it is something that is done by students." (Zimmerman and Schunk, 1989).

We do not learn by being told; or rather we may seem to learn but it is a surface learning - verbal learning - which is quickly forgotten and cannot readily be retrieved or applied to novel situations outside the context in which it was taught. We learn through action and interaction - interaction with the material to be mastered, with the teacher, with peers and with oneself. The role of assessment is to support this interactive process.

On this view, contexts for learning and contexts for assessment cannot be separated. If assessment procedures are designed to fit in with learning objectives, this linkage can be turned to advantage. If they are not (and the results are perceived as important), assessment still influences learning but it is the assessment objectives which are dominant.

However, educational decisions are not made on theoretical grounds such as these. Provision for assessment must take account of efficiency of operation as well as questions of validity and effects on classroom practice. Many of the alternative procedures are costly in teachers' (and pupils') time and effort. Whereas multiple-choice tests are relatively cheap and their results are easy to handle, open-ended questions and extended writing cost more to mark and are able to sample a smaller segment of the curriculum. In most countries, the marking of pupils' work is accepted as part of the teacher's job, often outside regular working hours. The use of portfolios may add substantially to the teacher's workload; schemes for "moderating" teachers' assessments by second marking or between schools are demanding on time. With inevitably limited resources, increased expenditure or time spent on one aspect means less available for others; do we already devote too much to assessment, and what is the appropriate proportion of expenditure to allocate to it? Although alternative assessment does not distinguish sharply between assessment and learning in this way, the question is still relevant.

However, the main obstacles to a wider acceptance of alternative assessment are connected with public attitudes and expectations. In countries where grades from tests or examinations have become accepted currency for judging individuals, and where school-based assessments and teachers' judgements are not part of the "assessment culture", doubts about the credibility of alternative assessment and suspicions of bias have still to be overcome. This applies not only at the stages where important decisions are made - for certification, selection and guidance - but also throughout the school years, when parents expect regular (and usually comparative) information about the standards achieved by their children and by the school. Teachers also may seek reassurance on these issues.

Conclusions

A recurring theme in this review is the range of functions which assessment is required to perform. For each of these functions, modes of assessment have been developed which meet these requirements reasonably well. The compromise solution which has emerged in an unplanned way is to use a variety of assessment practices to serve these different functions. But there is an inherent conflict. If assessment is revised in line with trends in curriculum reform - for "instructional improvement" (Chapter 8) - then it will move towards descriptive, non-judgemental, non-labelling procedures which support the teaching-learning process, closely tied to work done in individual classrooms and with individual pupils and relying mainly on teachers' judgements. This style of assessment is weak in ensuring appropriate coverage of the curriculum, and does not readily yield scores which can be used normatively to assess trends in standards. In contrast, accountability testing is an imposed coercive system, requiring comparable, communicable, standardized grades. It is an external device concerned primarily with control, whereas the alternative mode is essentially an internal procedure aiming at growth. If accountability testing were limited to samples only, at relatively infrequent intervals, it could run in parallel with less formal, instructional assessment. But the demand for accountability (in its widest sense) is not limited to periodic national monitoring: it necessarily extends to individual assessment -- for example to meet certification requirements - and at this level the requirements of control and growth come into conflict.

They conflict because of the climates of learning created by the two contrasting approaches. In discussing assessment systems, we tend to focus on issues of organisation and technique, neglecting the affective and social factors involved in learning. This is a common fault throughout education: we treat learning as intellectual and rational, and neglect the feelings and attitudes which determine what use we make of our knowledge, and even affect whether we learn or not. Acquiring knowledge is not enough: we also have to want to use that knowledge, and to want to continue learning. Teachers have always been aware of the importance of motivation: the more open and informal the system, the more important motivation is. A major factor which influences motivation in learning is our self-image, the perceptions we have of our own competence, in relation to the task and the social context. Self-image affects our response to difficulty: the confident learner is better able to persevere than one who has a self-image of inadequacy. If we see failure as due to lack of effort, we try harder; if we see it as due to our lack of ability, we give up. Building appropriate attitudes, to learning and to oneself, is a crucial part in teaching and learning.

Thus, in addition to its direct effect in publicly defining which pupils are regarded as successful or inadequate and which aspects of knowledge and skills are regarded as central or peripheral, assessment has a powerful indirect effect on attitudes and values within the learning process. It influences the disposition to learn, to further one's learning, to use strategies of thinking, to accept the value of rational argument and sound knowledge, to derive satisfaction from problem-solving and critical reasoning. Positive attitudes develop from relationships and models, are encouraged in a climate of learning which is tolerant of questioning and exploration, and are discouraged by an emphasis on memorising and an authoritative regime. De Corte (1990) argues for a balance of requirements, to create

> "powerful learning environments... characterised by a good balance between discovery learning and personal exploration on the one hand, and systematic instruction and guidance on the other."

Assessment is an important factor in creating or changing this climate. This affective dimension of assessment has not been adequately researched, but it is attracting increasing attention. In a review of European research on the teaching of thinking and reasoning skills, McGuinness and Nisbet (1991) note:

> "Researchers are looking for a more situated view of learning and instruction which includes not only cognitive factors, but affective, motivational and social influences as well."

Consequently, one of the criteria for judging an assessment system is therefore its impact on the climate of learning within the educational provision.

Assessment, like management, has to be concerned with both control and growth. The Educational Testing Service (1990) forecasts that "Educational testing will change more in the next ten years than it has done in the past fifty years." It is important that its development should not be a separate issue but be planned as an integral element in the context of curriculum reform.

REFERENCES

AUSTRALIAN SCHOOLS COMMISSION (1973), *Schools in Australia* (The Karmel Report). Canberra: Australian Government Printing Service.

BENNIS, W. G., BENNE, K. D. and CHIN, R. (1966), *The Planning of Change*. New York: Holt, Rinehart and Winston.

DE CORTE, E. (1990), "Towards powerful learning environments for the acquisition of problem-solving skills", *European Journal of Psychology*, 5, pp. 5-19.

ECKSTEIN, M. A. and NOAH, H. J. (1989a), "Forms and functions of secondary-school-leaving examinations", *Comparative Education*, 33, pp. 295-316.

ECKSTEIN, M. A. and NOAH, H. J. (1989b), "Trade-offs in examination policies: an international comparative perspective", *Oxford Review of Education*, 15, pp. 17-27.

ETS, Educational Testing Service (1990), "Helping America Raise Educational Standards for the 21st Century: 1990 Annual Report". Princeton: ETS.

HARGREAVES, A. (1989), *Curriculum and Assessment Reform*. Milton Keynes: Open University Press.

KELLAGHAN, T. and Madaus, G. F. (1991), "National testing: lessons for America from Europe", *Educational Leadership*, 49 (3), pp. 87-93.

McGUINNESS, C. and NISBET, J. (1991), "Teaching thinking in Europe", *British Journal of Educational Psychology*, 61, pp. 174-186.

ZIMMERMAN, B. J. and SCHUNK, D. H. (eds.) (1989), *Self-regulated Learning and Academic Achievement: Theory, Research and Practice*. New York: Springer-Verlag.

MAIN SALES OUTLETS OF OECD PUBLICATIONS
PRINCIPAUX POINTS DE VENTE DES PUBLICATIONS DE L'OCDE

ARGENTINA – ARGENTINE
Carlos Hirsch S.R.L.
Galería Güemes, Florida 165, 4° Piso
1333 Buenos Aires Tel. (1) 331.1787 y 331.2391
Telefax: (1) 331.1787

AUSTRALIA – AUSTRALIE
D.A. Information Services
648 Whitehorse Road, P.O.B 163
Mitcham, Victoria 3132 Tel. (03) 873.4411
Telefax: (03) 873.5679

AUSTRIA – AUTRICHE
Gerold & Co.
Graben 31
Wien I Tel. (0222) 533.50.14

BELGIUM – BELGIQUE
Jean De Lannoy
Avenue du Roi 202
B-1060 Bruxelles Tel. (02) 538.51.69/538.08.41
Telefax: (02) 538.08.41

CANADA
Renouf Publishing Company Ltd.
1294 Algoma Road
Ottawa, ON K1B 3W8 Tel. (613) 741.4333
Telefax: (613) 741.5439
Stores:
61 Sparks Street
Ottawa, ON K1P 5R1 Tel. (613) 238.8985
211 Yonge Street
Toronto, ON M5B 1M4 Tel. (416) 363.3171

Les Éditions La Liberté Inc.
3020 Chemin Sainte-Foy
Sainte-Foy, PQ G1X 3V6 Tel. (418) 658.3763
Telefax: (418) 658.3763

Federal Publications
165 University Avenue
Toronto, ON M5H 3B8 Tel. (416) 581.1552
Telefax: (416) 581.1743

Les Publications Fédérales
1185 Avenue de l'Université
Montréal, PQ H3B 3A7 Tel. (514) 954.1633
Telefax: (514) 954.1633

CHINA – CHINE
China National Publications Import
Export Corporation (CNPIEC)
16 Gongti E. Road, Chaoyang District
P.O. Box 88 or 50
Beijing 100704 PR Tel. (01) 506.6688
Telefax: (01) 506.3101

DENMARK – DANEMARK
Munksgaard Export and Subscription Service
35, Nørre Søgade, P.O. Box 2148
DK-1016 København K Tel. (33) 12.85.70
Telefax: (33) 12.93.87

FINLAND – FINLANDE
Akateeminen Kirjakauppa
Keskuskatu 1, P.O. Box 128
00100 Helsinki Tel. (358 0) 12141
Telefax: (358 0) 121.4441

FRANCE
OECD/OCDE
Mail Orders/Commandes par correspondance:
2, rue André-Pascal
75775 Paris Cedex 16 Tel. (33-1) 45.24.82.00
Telefax: (33-1) 45.24.81.76 or (33-1) 45.24.85.00
Telex: 640048 OCDE

OECD Bookshop/Librairie de l'OCDE :
33, rue Octave-Feuillet
75016 Paris Tel. (33-1) 45.24.81.67
(33-1) 45.24.81.81

Documentation Française
29, quai Voltaire
75007 Paris Tel. 40.15.70.00
Gibert Jeune (Droit-Économie)
6, place Saint-Michel
75006 Paris Tel. 43.25.91.19
Librairie du Commerce International
10, avenue d'Iéna
75016 Paris Tel. 40.73.34.60
Librairie Dunod
Université Paris-Dauphine
Place du Maréchal de Lattre de Tassigny
75016 Paris Tel. 47.27.18.56
Librairie Lavoisier
11, rue Lavoisier
75008 Paris Tel. 42.65.39.95
Librairie L.G.D.J. - Montchrestien
20, rue Soufflot
75005 Paris Tel. 46.33.89.85
Librairie des Sciences Politiques
30, rue Saint-Guillaume
75007 Paris Tel. 45.48.36.02
P.U.F.
49, boulevard Saint-Michel
75005 Paris Tel. 43.25.83.40
Librairie de l'Université
12a, rue Nazareth
13100 Aix-en-Provence Tel. (16) 42.26.18.08
Documentation Française
165, rue Garibaldi
69003 Lyon Tel. (16) 78.63.32.23
Librairie Decitre
29, place Bellecour
69002 Lyon Tel. (16) 72.40.54.54

GERMANY – ALLEMAGNE
OECD Publications and Information Centre
August-Bebel-Allee 6
D-W 5300 Bonn 2 Tel. (0228) 959.120
Telefax: (0228) 959.12.17

GREECE – GRÈCE
Librairie Kauffmann
Mavrokordatou 9
106 78 Athens Tel. 322.21.60
Telefax: 363.39.67

HONG-KONG
Swindon Book Co. Ltd.
13–15 Lock Road
Kowloon, Hong Kong Tel. 366.80.31
Telefax: 739.49.75

HUNGARY – HONGRIE
Euro Info Service
kázmér u.45
1121 Budapest Tel. (1) 182.00.44
Telefax : (1) 182.00.44

ICELAND – ISLANDE
Mál Mog Menning
Laugavegi 18, Pósthólf 392
121 Reykjavik Tel. 162.35.23

INDIA – INDE
Oxford Book and Stationery Co.
Scindia House
New Delhi 110001 Tel.(11) 331.5896/5308
Telefax: (11) 332.5993
17 Park Street
Calcutta 700016 Tel. 240832

INDONESIA – INDONÉSIE
Pdii-Lipi
P.O. Box 269/JKSMG/88
Jakarta 12790 Tel. 583467
Telex: 62 875

IRELAND – IRLANDE
TDC Publishers – Library Suppliers
12 North Frederick Street
Dublin 1 Tel. 74.48.35/74.96.77
Telefax: 74.84.16

ISRAEL
Electronic Publications only
Publications électroniques seulement
Sophist Systems Ltd.
71 Allenby Street
Tel-Aviv 65134 Tel. 3-29.00.21
Telefax: 3-29.92.39

ITALY – ITALIE
Libreria Commissionaria Sansoni
Via Duca di Calabria 1/1
50125 Firenze Tel. (055) 64.54.15
Telefax: (055) 64.12.57
Via Bartolini 29
20155 Milano Tel. (02) 36.50.83
Editrice e Libreria Herder
Piazza Montecitorio 120
00186 Roma Tel. 679.46.28
Telefax: 678.47.51
Libreria Hoepli
Via Hoepli 5
20121 Milano Tel. (02) 86.54.46
Telefax: (02) 805.28.86
Libreria Scientifica
Dott. Lucio de Biasio 'Aeiou'
Via Coronelli, 6
20146 Milano Tel. (02) 48.95.45.52
Telefax: (02) 48.95.45.48

JAPAN – JAPON
OECD Publications and Information Centre
Landic Akasaka Building
2-3-4 Akasaka, Minato-ku
Tokyo 107 Tel. (81.3) 3586.2016
Telefax: (81.3) 3584.7929

KOREA – CORÉE
Kyobo Book Centre Co. Ltd.
P.O. Box 1658, Kwang Hwa Moon
Seoul Tel. 730.78.91
Telefax: 735.00.30

MALAYSIA – MALAISIE
Co-operative Bookshop Ltd.
University of Malaya
P.O. Box 1127, Jalan Pantai Baru
59700 Kuala Lumpur
Malaysia Tel. 756.5000/756.5425
Telefax: 757.3661

MEXICO – MEXIQUE
Revistas y Periodicos Internacionales S.A. de C.V.
Florencia 57 - 1004
Mexico, D.F. 06600 Tel. 207.81.00
Telefax : 208.39.79

NETHERLANDS – PAYS-BAS
SDU Uitgeverij
Christoffel Plantijnstraat 2
Postbus 20014
2500 EA's-Gravenhage Tel. (070 3) 78.99.11
Voor bestellingen: Tel. (070 3) 78.98.80
Telefax: (070 3) 47.63.51

**NEW ZEALAND
NOUVELLE-ZÉLANDE**
Legislation Services
P.O. Box 12418
Thorndon, Wellington Tel. (04) 496.5652
Telefax: (04) 496.5698

NORWAY – NORVÈGE
Narvesen Info Center – NIC
Bertrand Narvesens vei 2
P.O. Box 6125 Etterstad
0602 Oslo 6 Tel. (02) 57.33.00
Telefax: (02) 68.19.01

PAKISTAN
Mirza Book Agency
65 Shahrah Quaid-E-Azam
Lahore 54000 Tel. (42) 353.601
Telefax: (42) 231.730

PHILIPPINE – PHILIPPINES
International Book Center
5th Floor, Filipinas Life Bldg.
Ayala Avenue
Metro Manila Tel. 81.96.76
Telex 23312 RHP PH

PORTUGAL
Livraria Portugal
Rua do Carmo 70-74
Apart. 2681
1117 Lisboa Codex Tel.: (01) 347.49.82/3/4/5
Telefax: (01) 347.02.64

SINGAPORE – SINGAPOUR
Information Publications Pte. Ltd.
41, Kallang Pudding, No. 04-03
Singapore 1334 Tel. 741.5166
Telefax: 742.9356

SPAIN – ESPAGNE
Mundi-Prensa Libros S.A.
Castelló 37, Apartado 1223
Madrid 28001 Tel. (91) 431.33.99
Telefax: (91) 575.39.98

Libreria Internacional AEDOS
Consejo de Ciento 391
08009 – Barcelona Tel. (93) 488.34.92
Telefax: (93) 487.76.59

Llibreria de la Generalitat
Palau Moja
Rambla dels Estudis, 118
08002 – Barcelona
(Subscripcions) Tel. (93) 318.80.12
(Publicacions) Tel. (93) 302.67.23
Telefax: (93) 412.18.54

SRI LANKA
Centre for Policy Research
c/o Colombo Agencies Ltd.
No. 300-304, Galle Road
Colombo 3 Tel. (1) 574240, 573551-2
Telefax: (1) 575394, 510711

SWEDEN – SUÈDE
Fritzes Fackboksföretaget
Box 16356
Regeringsgatan 12
103 27 Stockholm Tel. (08) 690.90.90
Telefax: (08) 20.50.21

Subscription Agency-Agence d'abonnements
Wennergren-Williams AB
P.O. Box 1305
171 25 Solna Tél. (08) 705.97.50
Téléfax : (08) 27.00.71

SWITZERLAND – SUISSE
Maditec S.A. (Books and Periodicals - Livres
et périodiques)
Chemin des Palettes 4
Case postale 2066
1020 Renens 1 Tel. (021) 635.08.65
Telefax: (021) 635.07.80

Librairie Payot S.A.
4, place Pépinet
1003 Lausanne Tel. (021) 341.33.48
Telefax: (021) 341.33.45

Librairie Unilivres
6, rue de Candolle
1205 Genève Tel. (022) 320.26.23
Telefax: (022) 329.73.18

Subscription Agency - Agence d'abonnement
Dynapresse Marketing S.A.
38 avenue Vibert
1227 Carouge Tel.: (022) 308.07.89
Telefax : (022) 308.07.99

See also – Voir aussi :
OECD Publications and Information Centre
August-Bebel-Allee 6
D-W 5300 Bonn 2 (Germany) Tel. (0228) 959.120
Telefax: (0228) 959.12.17

TAIWAN – FORMOSE
Good Faith Worldwide Int'l. Co. Ltd.
9th Floor, No. 118, Sec. 2
Chung Hsiao E. Road
Taipei Tel. (02) 391.7396/391.7397
Telefax: (02) 394.9176

THAILAND – THAÏLANDE
Suksit Siam Co. Ltd.
113, 115 Fuang Nakhon Rd.
Opp. Wat Rajbopith
Bangkok 10200 Tel. (662) 251.1630
Telefax: (662) 236.7783

TURKEY – TURQUIE
Kültür Yayinlari Is-Türk Ltd. Sti.
Atatürk Bulvari No. 191/Kat 13
Kavaklidere/Ankara Tel. 428.11.40 Ext. 2458
Dolmabahce Cad. No. 29
Besiktas/Istanbul Tel. 260.71.88
Telex: 43482B

UNITED KINGDOM – ROYAUME-UNI
HMSO
Gen. enquiries Tel. (071) 873 0011
Postal orders only:
P.O. Box 276, London SW8 5DT
Personal Callers HMSO Bookshop
49 High Holborn, London WC1V 6HB
Telefax: (071) 873 8200
Branches at: Belfast, Birmingham, Bristol, Edinburgh, Manchester

UNITED STATES – ÉTATS-UNIS
OECD Publications and Information Centre
2001 L Street N.W., Suite 700
Washington, D.C. 20036-4910 Tel. (202) 785.6323
Telefax: (202) 785.0350

VENEZUELA
Libreria del Este
Avda F. Miranda 52, Aptdo. 60337
Edificio Galipán
Caracas 106 Tel. 951.1705/951.2307/951.1297
Telegram: Libreste Caracas

Subscription to OECD periodicals may also be placed through main subscription agencies.

Les abonnements aux publications périodiques de l'OCDE peuvent être souscrits auprès des principales agences d'abonnement.

Orders and inquiries from countries where Distributors have not yet been appointed should be sent to: OECD Publications Service, 2 rue André-Pascal, 75775 Paris Cedex 16, France.

Les commandes provenant de pays où l'OCDE n'a pas encore désigné de distributeur devraient être adressées à : OCDE, Service des Publications, 2, rue André-Pascal, 75775 Paris Cedex 16, France.

02-1993